The Local State

'compulsory reading for anyone who is concerned to understand the problems of our inner cities' *Roof* (Shelter)

'an important and original book' *New Society*

'the power of its argument is compelling . . . worthy of Engels' *The Guardian*

Cynthia Cockburn

The Local State
Management of Cities and People

Pluto  Press

Second impression 1978
First published 1977 by Pluto Press Limited
Unit 10 Spencer Court, 7 Chalcot Road, London NW1 8LH

0 904383 48 2 paperback
0 904383 49 0 hardback

Cover design by Tom Sullivan

Printed and bound in Great Britain at
The Camelot Press Limited, Southampton

Contents

Introduction

In the London Borough of Lambeth hundreds of houses belonging to the council have been closed up with corrugated iron. Pasted across some of them is a poster which reads 'More and more people are coming to realise that Lambeth Planning Department are wreckers'. The message comes from local people. It arises from the fact that while there are many thousand families waiting for council tenancies and several hundred actually homeless, yet the council is deliberately smashing and boarding up houses that could be made habitable. Indeed, in some cases the council have had to remove people from these houses so that workmen could go in and break them up; people who were prepared, for want of anything better, to live there. A council destroying its own property – what could be more perverse.

There are many such anomalies in local government. People will tell you how local authorities are given more and more official jobs to do, spend more money every year, and yet the same people are certain that 'local democracy is at risk'. Councils redevelop their areas to provide houses for local people and by so doing exacerbate a decline in local jobs and incomes. Housing departments evict families from council flats for falling into arrears and the next day have to fulfil their statutory obligation to rehouse them. The research that underlies this book was directed towards understanding how such contradictions arise.

Local government is normally understood as being like a vehicle. If the working class manage to seize the wheel by winning an election it will go where they choose to steer it. The fact that experience shows time and again that this does not happen, that Labour councils are little more able than Conservative councils to respond to the interests of the local working class is seldom allowed to shake two beliefs: that the vehicle is obediently in the command of whoever sits in the electoral driver's seat, and that when Labour does so, the people do. To understand any of these contradictions means moving into another frame of reference and seeing local government from quite a different viewpoint. It means recognising that our local councils don't spring from some ancient right of self-government but are, and under capitalism have always been, an aspect of national government which in turn is a part of the state. It means expecting to find a practical connection between the work the state does (local councils included) and the way wealth is produced in our society. It also means seeing that the services which we ourselves need and struggle to win from the state must also be seen as 'servicing', we are serviced for our labour power.

The question I've chosen to examine more closely is the relationship between two new trends in local government: *corporate management* and *community development*. Many local authorities, especially those in big cities, have been undergoing a modernisation of their management systems designed to give them tighter control over their finance and over their workforce, together with a more powerful impact on urban life through their policies. Yet at the same time as pursuing corporate management they have been encouraging democratic control through 'participation'; opening up the council doors; offering support to community organisation. Central government has prompted and assisted both reforms. Do corporate management and community development pull in opposite directions – or are they the tough and the tender aspects of one principle: management?

A good deal of contemporary research, with warm-hearted intentions, studies working-class groups and situations on behalf of those who make policy. This book begins with a different point of view about political change: that it stems from the working class. So this is a study of urban managers and urban management situations and techniques from the viewpoint of those who are managed.

The study is based on three years' research carried out as a member of the staff of the Centre for Environmental Studies. The views expressed here, though, are mine and should not be taken to reflect those of the Centre. I am grateful to those elected members and officers in Lambeth and other councils who spent time with me talking about their experiences of council work. I hope it will be clear that my study is one of a situation and a structure and not one of personalities. It may seem that the picture of Lambeth unfolded here underestimates the amount that people in the council give, how much they take on themselves the problem of deprivation. That is not so. It is *precisely because* of the caring and commitment of so many elected members and officers that it is important to understand the exact nature of the institution in which they work. Callousness played a smaller part in the wrecking of Lambeth's council houses than it is sometimes thought.

There are many who will disagree with this analysis. The Leader of the Labour Party group with a majority on Lambeth Borough Council at the time of my research there has commented on the manuscript: 'I disagree with many of the inferences drawn and consider you have been very selective in the material used in order to bolster-up a pre-determined conclusion reached before we accorded facilities to you.' Such differences cannot be avoided. I was at pains to hear the expression of many contrasted points of view. I interviewed more than sixty people in the borough, inside and outside the town hall, some of them twice. Many of the interviews lasted two or three hours. My account does not introduce any conflict that was not inherent in the local situation as it was revealed in those conversations.

I would like to thank the several people who have helped look after my children while I have worked – particularly Jillie, without whom I would not have begun, let alone finished, the project.

To *thank* the ten or twelve people who worked closely with me over successive drafts of the book would be to set them apart from it in some way, as though this were more my own than in fact it is. It has been a shared piece of work and was the subject of many conversations. All of us who discussed its content were aware of many other people struggling with the same theme: people organising politically around such issues as housing, health and social welfare; workers in local authorities and other state agencies questioning their own role and that of their employers; students; local councillors; and many people, women particularly, examining more closely the link between state and family.

The book is put forward, not as a water-tight statement, but as notes that might be of momentary use in discussions of practice.

1. Gearing up to govern

Officialdom in Lambeth lives in a Victorian town hall that dominates the junction between Brixton Hill and Acre Lane. From the steps of the main entrance you can look across to the 'Prince of Wales' where the West Indian regulars congregate outside. On the other corner is Times Furnishing, where they take down-payments and forward promises in exchange for three-piece suites. In Lambeth it is easier to get a three-piece suite than a flat to put it in. Inside the town hall the local officials have their rooms along the handsome tiled corridors, and in a theatrical council chamber meets the body of men and women, elected by the people, who are supposed, according to the theory of liberal democracy, to impose their will on the bureaucracy.

Lambeth town hall has seen a few changes in its time. Once the seat of the council of the old Metropolitan Borough of Lambeth it has been, since 1964, the headquarters of an authority two or three times as big. Its functions long ago spilled over into office blocks, stores and workshops throughout the district. In April 1968, however, changes began to occur inside the town hall that were of a different kind, and at first were scarcely visible to the outside world. They had a significance for the people on Brixton's pavements, but it was not something of which they were aware.

The 'management revolution' in Lambeth Borough Council was begun by the Tory majority that came to power in the 1968 elections. The council chamber had been dominated for thirty years by the Labour Party. Lambeth and Labour went together like fish and chips. When the Tories entered the town hall as its political leadership the morning after the election, no less surprised by the size of their majority than the Labour Party by the scale of its defeat, they took on a council with an annual turnover of nearly £16 million. To it they brought a natural inclination for business efficiency and tight purse-strings.

Three years later, when the Conservatives ceded their place to Labour once again, the balance of authority and the nature of council decision-making had changed quite strikingly. What had existed as a loose assembly of council committees and a multiplicity of small departments, their work barely co-ordinated, had become a tightly-knit hierarchy under the control of a board of powerful directors, in close partnership with a top-level caucus of majority party members. The town clerk had gone, and in his place was a chief executive, the corporate manager. An annual cycle of conscious, analytical forward planning had been set in train.

The senior officers feared that the returning Labour group would reverse this new management set-up. But the Labour Party too had changed. The incoming Labour leader of 1971 was an economics teacher. Many of his colleagues, whose average age was undoubtedly the youngest ever known in this council, were not manual workers but professional and managerial people to whom the new ways came naturally. The Labour group took on and developed the management structure left by the Tories. The system that existed in 1974 was thus the product of both political parties and the local bureaucracy. The formula, however, came from elsewhere: from the world of big business.

Control in business enterprise

At its most simple, corporate management means 'managing things as a whole', taking an overall view of an institution, whether it is a hospital, a company or a local authority, deciding what it should do and guiding its activities towards achieving these purposes, bearing in mind probable changes in the outside world. It is 'intelligent' behaviour in institutions. One might then wonder why such a concept as corporate management in local government is worth studying, since we could assume that most people responsible for organisations want them to survive and grow and achieve their goals and are bound to use their wits to see it happens. The significance of management, though, differs from one institution to another and is specific to different periods of history and different kinds of society. It is not because management of itself is good or bad, but because big business and local government have a bearing on the interests of ordinary people, that corporate management is worth examining.

The moment when a new style of management is looked for is the moment when existing means of control are under pressure. The failure of old ways of doing things is sometimes brought about by an internal crisis in a company. A manager may feel a need for corporate management when a build-up of pressure from one or other element in the operation brings the firm to crisis point. In a company this can be loss of profitability or an abrupt change in technology, some new invention which forces a choice between risky investment in new machinery or a sudden switch in the place the company is trying to fill in the market. It can also be sparked off by a recognition that an organisation has grown in size and complexity to the point at which it has crossed a threshold and become unmanageable by existing methods. As a multi-operation company expands, the different factors a manager has to hold in his head and use in decision-making grow in number too and their inter-relationships grow even more rapidly. His control is threatened.*

To govern such a complex system the manager can be helped by certain 'hard' management aids, such as computers which can simplify the analysis of a growing mass of data. There are many discrete techniques he can use such as work study,[1] job evaluation or linear programming. An early stage in the managerial revolution was the introduction of somewhat more comprehensive scientific disciplines for the study and maintenance of 'complex man-machine systems', as the jargon calls a production company.

---

* The masculine pronoun reflects the fact that nearly all business managers are men. It is not used neutrally.

Operations research for example grew out of war-time military planning. Management by objectives (MbO) entered British business in the late fifties and early sixties: GKN and Smiths Ltd. were leaders in 'developing a hierarchical system of objective setting'.[2] United States management consultancy firms with branches operating in the UK were instrumental in bringing such new techniques to British industry.

Corporate management, as such, however, represents more than the sum of these management tools. It is called by its exponents 'a marriage of management and science'. It looks at the system as a whole, its goals, strategies and growth. It has regard to the pattern of relationships within an organisation to ensure efficient flows of information; to defining channels of responsibility and accountability − for whom you answer and to whom; to the design of decision-processes so that different types of decision are taken at appropriate levels and in appropriate sequences.

The practice of corporate management was established in large British firms during the 1960s. It had been introduced first in the USA in the late 1950s. We get an indication of the pace of growth from John Argenti's estimate[3] that in 1968 it was 'being used, in one form or another, in several hundred companies there [i.e. in the USA]. In Britain only a few dozen are yet using it and only very few have been doing so for more than three or four years.' Somewhere, then, around 1960 corporate management began to reach British business.

Two trends in British capital go some way to explain why an increasing number of businesses took on board corporate management and planning in this period. The first is the striking concentration of manufacturing industry that had been occurring since the pre-war period but was particularly accentuated from the 1950s. This tendency to monopoly occurs within an industry as big firms buy up small, or arrange mergers with other sizeable companies. The annual rate of change in concentration in British industries multiplied four-fold between the period 1935−51 and the period 1963−68. A growing number of industries showed signs of a gathering of business into fewer and fewer hands. During the decade 1958–68 the rate of change was consistently high. Many firms were diversifying too and buying into industries other than their original one – so the rate quoted above certainly under-represents the reality.[4] There was a tendency in the sixties also for companies increasingly to own capital investments in foreign companies and for foreign companies to own interests in British firms. This of course represents the growth of large corporations spanning over and above national borders. In the UK the propor-tion of external assets in total assets doubled, and the proportion of UK liabilities that were external trebled between 1962 and 1968.[5]

The scale and complexity of the firms that result from such concentration demand systems-management of a far more advanced kind than is needed by smallscale competitive capital. Corporate management is the way of life of the decision-makers in the international monopolies.[6]

The shift to the new ways of managing is not always or only provoked by a growth-crisis. Firms can be threatened by loss of profitability. A concurrent economic trend in Britain in the sixties was a steady decline in levels of profitability in many industries, in spite of overall growth in the Gross National Product. It has been suggested[7] that this profit squeeze was brought about by a pincer movement of foreign competition and loss of imperial advantages on the one hand, and worker pressure on wages on the other. Certainly in the sixties the British working class began to test their new strength, fortified by relatively full employment, a shortage of skilled labour in some industries and areas, and more adequate social security, factors which 'militated against discipline at work' and made labour unpredictability a growing problem to managements.[8]

The government too, responsible for the health of the economy as a whole, had an interest in beefing up British management. During the sixties it was becoming clear that Britain's economic perform-ance was lagging behind that of her European competitors. The nagging balance of payments crisis, due to the failure of British firms to export sufficiently, was leading to alarming doubts about the ability of managers in British industry. 'The country's general loss of economic self-confidence may have been reflected in businessmen becoming less resistant to criticism or to suggestion coming from the academic world.'[9] Ideas long established in American business schools began to penetrate British higher education. Before the second world war management education barely existed here, nor did the post-war decade see much change in this. But in 1965 business schools were founded in London and Manchester, and courses in other universities quickly followed. Top management showed itself readier to take on new recruits trained in modern methods and indeed to go back to school themselves. Often the new ideas were introduced into the company by management consultants, professional firms within the business system that had seen a profit to be made in helping others to improve their profitability.[10] Academics too were involved, not only in management-development as such, but in applying sociology and psychology in the new field of organisation studies and other disciplines devised mainly for use in industry and commerce.

A corpus of academic management science grew to meet the demand. The trainee manager at college learned corporate planning.[11] He learned how to specify the company's objectives and goals – what it was meaning to achieve; how to select policies and programmes to achieve it; how to determine the type and amount of resources required and how they could be obtained and allocated to different activities. He learned how to design and operate within sophisticated management systems affording sensitive controls, procedures for anticipating or correcting errors or failures in the corporation's plans.[12] Using systems theory and cybernetics the firm could be understood as an analogue of the brain and nervous system itself. The ultimate aim was to achieve controls in the firm as subtle and adaptive as those of the human body.[13]

This was the school of thought that was also, indirectly, tutoring British local government. Needless to say, most local councils in general and the London Borough of Lambeth in particular, fall about as far short of the ideal corporate scheme as a rowing boat does of a nuclear submarine. But then, so do most private businesses as well. Only the giants, the monopolies and perhaps the armed forces of powerful countries, have yet been driven by circumstances to utilise these sciences to the full, or had the resources to do so.

The transfer into local government

There is no direct route from ICI's boardroom to Lambeth town hall. Yet the principles and practices of corporate management and planning did travel from the business world into central and local government in the 1960s.

The nineteenth century had seen the gradual construction, by laws promulgated in Westminster and practices established in Whitehall, of a system of local government more or less adequate for an industrialising country. From the Municipal Corporations Act 1835 through to the creation of county councils in 1888 and district councils in 1894, the foundations of local government were being laid. In that form the structure stood for a while. From the beginning of this century for fifty or sixty years most of the changes that did occur were merely shifts in the level at which responsibilities were performed. Functions added to local government were sometimes those formerly carried out by central government or by ad hoc bodies such as school boards and Poor Law unions. Those lost, like the management of trunk roads and hospitals, went up to national government or to regional agencies. There had been, too, occasional transfers of function from one tier of local government to another, as when county councils acquired planning functions in the post-war period.

Then, in the late fifties, a period of structural development more akin to that of the previous century began. As the official architects of the reforms made clear, they too were impelled by economic changes. Industrial development, population growth and a dramatic increase in the use of motor transport had caused towns to spill out far beyond the boundaries of the authorities meant to govern them. For a start much larger authorities were needed. Existing authorities were 'too small in terms of area, population and resources, including highly qualified manpower and technical equipment' for the job they had to do, wrote Lord Redcliffe-Maud.[14] Since the war the government had 'had to assume far more direct responsibility for the management of the economy'.[15] Modernisation was overdue. 'There is an evident contrast between this enormous increase in the activities of government and the extent and pace of change in the government institutions' wrote the authors of the Kilbrandon Report on the Constitution.[16]

The changes in local government between 1957 and 1974 have brought into existence a radically new pattern of local authorities. They are different from the old in their boundaries, in the share-out of functions and in the way they go about their work. It was the *internal* management reforms of local authorities that were called corporate management and planning. But the *external* reforms were based on the same principles, carried out through similar vehicles and derived from much the same sources as the internal measures. In part, the more far-reaching restructuring was brought about to enable this new, more rational, approach within the bodies responsible for urban and local management. Certainly, without new ways of doing things inside the new authorities there would have been little point for the state to undertake such extensive (and expensive) changes. Besides, one of the principles of corporate management and planning within authorities, certainly within local councils, was to introduce a capability that would span the gap between different state bodies at local level and so help to co-ordinate the work of the separate new authorities into a single coherent system of government. The system as a whole was being geared up to govern more intrusively and more effectively.

The first major vehicle of reform was the Herbert Commission, set up in 1957 by a Conservative government to consider the organisation of local government in the London area. Most of its findings[17] were put into effect in the London Government Act 1963, which created the Greater London Council and the thirty-two London boroughs. This was the origin of the new Lambeth borough. In a sense, therefore, the management reform in Lambeth, began, not in 1968 with the advent of the Tories, but in 1963 with the creation of the new authority. It was born, so to speak, looking a good deal more corporate than the old Metropolitan Borough Council it replaced. The old council had had sixteen committees. An average member might have sat on three or four of these – he or she had to know about a fair number of aspects of the work of the council. The new council had only eleven main committees and an average member was sitting only on two or three. The corporate trend was under way. It involved, as elsewhere, centralisation, grouping of functions. It meant that gradually many little departments were consolidated into domains that had more responsibilities and were consequently stronger; that elected members specialised more in their council interests, were involved in fewer policy fields and in these more exclusively.

The reorganisation of London government was followed nine years later by the 1972 Act which swept away the 1,300 or more assorted English county, county borough, urban district and rural district councils that had served since the last century and replaced them with a uniform system of about 400 councils, arranged in a two-tier system of counties and districts. While the local government system was in the melting pot at least four official committees set about the study of the appropriate internal management methods of local authorities. 'Maud, Maud, Mallaby, Mallaby, Patterson, Bains all four', as the nursery rhyme was rewritten. Though the four reports differed in detail the principles were shared. As in business the message was: integration, control from the top, more efficient use of money and labour, forward planning for a bigger impact on the job in hand.[18]

Alongside the reform of the general-purpose elected local councils in this period attention was also given to more specific services. The Seebohm Committee on the social services (followed by an Act of Parliament in 1970) brought about a strengthening and rationalising of the management of social welfare.[19] A Water Act removed the job of water supply and sewage disposal from those local councils that had administered them in the past and created new local agencies: a system of regional and divisional water authorities 'responsible for the whole of the hydrological cycle'. The National Health Service was reorganised and an Act in 1973 created new regional and area health authorities which would take to themselves some of the work of the Department of Health and Social Security and of the Regional Hospital Boards, and remove from local councils their share of the personal health services. Both these reorganisations were accompanied by management studies that urged the new authorities to adopt a rational corporate management structure and co-ordinative planning, much as was intended in the new local councils.[20] During the period 1960–74 many similar recommendations were made, in differing degrees official, on other services, including transport, education, housing and the environment. It was a time of conscious reassessment of forms and styles of government.

Because local authorities have substantial control over their own internal working, the putting into action of the management reforms was not a matter for dictation. It was left to example and persuasion. Numerous government circulars urged the various new local bodies to adopt the management proposals, although allowing different interpretations of detail.[21] Professional corporate planners, trying to convert the local authorities to the new ways, wished very much that central government had been more dogmatic – it would have strengthened their hand within the town hall, where old ways died hard.

Legislation was involved, however, in the accompanying changes in town planning.[22] The local land-use planning of the forties and fifties was to give way in the big new authorities to a more comprehensive and longer-term strategic planning cycle, better able to use the analytical and predictive techniques being developed in the universities and research centres. In many ways the aims of the new structure planning, as it was called, matched those of corporate management: an overview of urban affairs. But it was complementary. Where corporate management, at least in the early days, looked inwards to the council's own resources, structure planning looked outwards to industry, land, housing and the environment. Many of the professionals concerned, both physical and corporate planners, looked for a marrying of the two.

The portrait that follows of corporate management as it took shape in Lambeth will illustrate without too much distortion the form it took in many local authorities. Though there were differences of detail from one council to another there were broad similarities of structure and intention.

The management story was, of course, not static. It unfolded over the period 1960 to 1974 both within a council like Lambeth and in Britain generally. It began, as in business before, as a matter of simple measures of administrative efficiency, with the introduction of distinct management techniques, cost-saving and productivity-raising devices. It was the age of initials: O and M (organisation & method), OR (operations research), CBA (cost-benefit analysis), CPA (critical path analysis) and many more, all backed up by that universal mother's help: the electronic computer. It was a time of steady increase in the rate bill, combined with staff shortages. Productivity was a key word in local government as in industrial relations at this time. Practical problems of redevelopment of the outworn city centres were taking over from the earlier pressures of reconstruction after the war. A Conservative government was trying to top the charts in house building. Councils were worried about the destruction of city life by the motor car. It is difficult to realise how unprecedented such *management* ideas, modest as they now seem, really were in those sleepy town and county halls where adequate administration had been the height of any Clerk's ambition.

The second phase of reform, beginning in the middle sixties, brought a switch from this efficiency-seeking phase, a concern with one task at a time, to a concern with the local authority *as a whole*. Its expression was the integrated management system. The recommendations of the Maud Committee on the Management of Local Government, published in 1967, were a thoroughgoing expression of the bid to remake councils in a corporate image.[23]

Not all of the Maud Report is concerned with management structure – but that was its main message. It recommended fewer committees and smaller committees – hence more specialisation of members' roles. It insisted that committees ought to be 'deliberative' rather than executive – hence giving officers more clear-cut scope for action. It recommended a management board of senior elected members, which would have wide powers delegated to it for formulating objectives, reviewing progress, maintaining overall supervision, presenting business to the full council and taking decisions on its behalf. Although Maud did not use the term 'chief executive' his re-styled Clerk to the Council was the CE in all but name. Unlike the old town clerk he was no longer to be 'first among equals'. Instead he should be 'undisputed head of the whole paid service of the council' and should be clearly senior to his team, which would be a small group of no more than six or seven principal officers. His job: 'effectiveness and efficiency of the organisation, and co-ordination (and integration where necessary) of its activities'. 'The guiding principle' should be 'that issues are dealt with at the lowest level consistent with the nature of the problem.' There was to be a clear separation of strategy from day to day decision making – this was the first sign of the corporate planning of the future.

In the past, local councils had been traditionally organised into semi-autonomous departments or services, each dominated by a particular profession. The education committee for instance was even called 'the education authority' – it thought of its buildings and its staff as its own, not those of the council. Such departmentalism and competitive professionalism were strongly criticised by the Maud report. A situation where the town clerk had to oversee 35 independent (and often warring) departments and as many committees was no design for effective government. The message was clear: *integrate*, through the related devices of 'horizontal' co-ordination and 'vertical' hierarchy. Sideways links were to be forged between the separate services. Up-down chains of accountability and responsibility were to be clarified and strengthened. 'A cleaner, tighter management of the local authority', as one corporate planner later put it. This would result, naturally, in a further division of labour between member and member, officer and officer, and between one and the other.

The Mallaby Report on staffing, published simultaneously with Maud, initiated manpower planning for the white-collar worker − the professionals and semi-professionals and office workers of the local state. It was part of the second phase of modernisation in management. 'A local authority should be regarded as an entity and its staff as the employees of the council as a whole rather than of individual committees . . . the authority has a duty to ensure that services are operated with the smallest number of staff consistent with the standard of service which the authority requires.' The report proposed the up-grading of 'establishment officers', which is the council's word for those in charge of personnel. For the first time the local authority employee was beginning to feel the cool wind of business management methods.[24]

Maud's management differs little from business management. The insistence is on strong control from the top. As Argenti[25] says, for the private firm 'corporate planning is concerned with problems of the kind that can only be tackled by the top levels of company management . . . its prime function is to examine and illuminate decisions on overall company strategy at the top'. It was a response to similar kinds of problem to those corporate management responded to in the business world: growing size and complexity of activities, the need for financial stringency. The second phase of local government management reform coincided with increasingly overt concern about levels of public spending.

A more subtle and adaptive approach to urban management was, however, on the way. The Maud concept of local government, however shattering an innovation it may have seemed to die-hard members or town clerks still believing in seat-of-the-pants management, fell a long way short of the ideas that were current seven or eight years later in 1974 or 1975. These Maud-style reforms of the late sixties while making gestures to the 'social environment' were basically still inward looking. They were concerned with resource management, a closer grip on money and personnel, with bringing efficiency to the whole authority as a unit of government. The Maud report was about corporate management – it was not about corporate planning. The committee's ideas on the decision-process were rudimentary and compare oddly with the zappy formulae of McKinsey and other consultants advising local government five years later.

It was around 1969 or 1970 that the management movement began to take on a new character, or rather that two aspects of it began to come to the fore.[26] This coincided with the 'rediscovery' of urban poverty and with increased working class militancy in cities. The first was, naturally, therefore a concern with the *outwardness* of the local state's activity, more appeal to 'community', environment, problem and purpose. The population joined the council's own employees as a twin subject of management.[27] The second aspect now underlined was *effectiveness*, an idea that has two faces, one about inputs and one about outputs. It is a question of the value you get, what you actually achieve, for the spending you make. If cost efficiency was important,[28] policy impact was becoming vital. The sights were raised: councils had to move from administration to government. They were being asked to solve problems out there 'in the community'.[29]

Once management structures had been reformed in the new upper and lower tier councils and in the water and health authorities, the way was open for corporate planning to act as the tool by which not just local councils but the *whole set* of local state institutions could achieve more impact through their policies on the areas they jointly governed.[30] A total approach to governance was being developed at an academic level. The Institute for Operational Research had for some years been working on an 'intelligent' planning process for local government, a process they called strategic choice.[31] This led to their most recent work on the *inter-corporate* dimension of public planning.[32] 'Corporate planning is not enough,' they wrote. 'Especially in the public sector . . . the making of strategic decisions must be considered not merely as a corporate but also as an inter-organisational process.' There were clear pressures to extend the processes of decision-making across the boundaries between government and business.[33] Not only could new planning processes forge a closer link between the interests of business and government, the very style of corporate management, the language that both partners were now speaking, brought them closer together.[34]

Led from the centre

One striking fact about this phase of contemporary history is the range and variety of official and semi-official institutions that played a part in it. The development of corporate management in local authorities amounts to a movement. The dominant role was that of central government, and of its ministries the Department of the Environment (DoE), directly responsible for local government, naturally took the lead. The DoE's very creation was a corporate reform, pulling into one integrated management the component ministries of transport, housing and local government plus some acquisitions from other departments too. The former Ministry of Housing and Local Government (MHLG) had masterminded the shift from town planning to structure planning. It was an initiative from MHLG and, eventually, MHLG funds, that set up and maintains the Centre for Environmental Studies which does research for urban and regional planning. It responded to the call of the national associations of local authorities in setting up the Maud, Mallaby and Bains committees and administered the local government reorganisation that followed the 1972 Act. DoE's influence can be seen in education and training for management. They encouraged the associations in forming a Local Government Training Board (LGTB) and gave financial support to their Local Authorities Management Services and Computer Committee (formed 1968). In turn, LGTB has sponsored upward of two thousand local government officers and members on the various short management courses it recognises. It was DoE that found the funds to set up the School of Advanced Urban Studies in Bristol, providing high-level seminars for officers and members. They also commissioned three consultant firms to make the 'urban guide-lines studies' of Sunderland, Rotherham and Oldham in 1972.[35]

The new management ideas fell on fertile ground – had it not been so they would never have taken root as they did. A reading of the local government journals over this period shows that there was a prolonged tussle inside local government over the movement towards integration and control. Though the impetus came from DoE it was not merely an imposition. Influential authorities and individual councillors and senior officers in the field supported corporate management. The lead for reform within the councils came from certain of the bigger authorities – or at least those that were big when measured by the problems they faced or the budgets they commanded. They began to innovate more or less independently and their experience made an impact on others. Among county councils, Cheshire gave a lead. Some of the big county boroughs such as Coventry and Liverpool were in the field early, and certain London boroughs, Lambeth among them. Those authorities that took an initiative usually did so through the push of a particular pioneering individual – a chief executive or treasurer ahead of his time. But where that was so, it was individuals who were closely linked to the outside world, who were at the top of their organisations, outward-looking, in touch with ministers, higher civil servants and academics, active in their professions. It did not come (with rare exceptions) from line managers responsible for individual services or from elected members intent mainly on a representational role. Among the local authority 'clubs', a keen promoter was the Association of Municipal Corporations as it was then known. The Institute of Municipal Treasurers and Account-ants pioneered management accountancy and financial planning for the public sector.[36]

If the ideas were to catch on, new skills and new apprecia-tions had to be taught. Universities and polytechnics were involved in the movement.[37] The Institute of Local Government Studies in the University of Birmingham began to become a kind of powerhouse of corporate thinking and management.[38] Many hundreds of local government officers and members, from middle management to the most influential leaders and chief executives, passed through Birmingham's campus, attending short courses, lecturing, joining in seminars. It became a forum for the discussion of these developments. The Institute of Local Government Studies in October 1971 began to publish its own journal[39] in response to 'the speed of the management revolution in local government and the challenges of reorganisation'. The journal aimed to provide information to help those responsible for local services and others involved in local decision-making to keep abreast of change. A number of sponsored local government management courses began in certain polytechnics and the LGTB published a recommendation on training for management.[40]

The management consultants were busy too. They had pioneered American management methods in British business. Now they saw a new market opening up in government. Central government used the private consultants to effect improvements in its own departments. First were those concerned with the armed forces, always more prone than others to think strategically. But the National Health Service, gas, electricity, British Airways and the BBC all at one time or another got the McKinsey treatment. Some of the local studies by consultants carried weight far beyond the borders of the local authorities to which they were addressed.[41] McKinsey and Co. Inc. in particular became specialists in local government affairs and published papers of a general kind on 'the problems of cities'.[42] Abreast of the times, their more recent work has been on the improvements of connecting mechanisms between state planning and planning in capitalist enterprise.

These management consultants were in most cases the same firms who were earning their bread-and-butter modernising the management systems of industry and commerce. They were thus clearly the nearest thing to a direct channel of ideas and methods from the business world to the local state. In fact, it is interesting that the business world, with this exception, was *not* the agent that converted local authorities to its own style of practice. There were some but relatively few representatives from private companies on the commissions and committees that studied the management problems of the local state. The company secretary of ICI who sat on the Bains Committee was one of a handful of business personalities that assisted in these reforms. Normally in these matters opinion is merely sounded through the Confederation of British Industry and other associations at one remove from the firm itself. Among the leading innovators Lord Seebohm is exceptional – confidently spanning two worlds. Architect of the modern social services, he has long also been involved at policy level with Barclays Bank Ltd, and is chairman of the Finance Corporation for Industry. More characteristically, this intermediary role is played by leading members of the professions, the apparently neutral stratum between government and business. J.P.R.Maud (later Lord Redcliffe-Maud) is a noted academic, civil servant and diplomat. Sir Edwin Herbert (Lord Tangley) was a solicitor whose practice was in the commercial life of the City of London.

There has been some direct transfusion of new blood into local government from industry, young men coming from company management or management sciences, people outside the normal local government professions.[43] In some cases this reflects the changing relationship of local authorities to local industry. The Community Land Act is a case in point: Southwark Borough Council for example has taken on specialists from property companies to fill the new roles it calls for. No doubt other councils will do so too. Ian Holden, author of a well-known book on 'planning for profit'[44] later got the job of Director of Industrial Development in the council at Hull. When transplants have been too abrupt, however, they have been rejected, as for instance the adoption of Frank Harris from Ford to the Newcastle City Corporation by a Labour council in 1965. While such new patterns of recruitment illustrate the changes we are observing, they are certainly not striking enough to have caused them. Even with the 1974 reorganisation there was not the influx of new officers from industry that was expected and feared by some. The reasons for the introduction of corporate management into local government are to be found not in personalities but in economic and political change.

Two questions remain. The first is to what extent at local level was corporate management an initiative by paid officials rather than by elected members? Informal evidence from the Association of Municipal Corporations and a reading of its journal over the critical period indicates that the main thrust for corporate management and planning has come from the officer side of local government. Indeed, there has always been anxiety about the effects of the new ways on the elected member and on political life in an authority. This is not to say that individual members have not been behind it – particularly dynamic leaders of councils such as T. Dan Smith in Newcastle and Bill Sefton in Liverpool. A rational management structure backed by management techniques and efficient information systems has room at the top for a strongman. And such a system no doubt suited their individual political goals. Without such supporters on the political side, corporate management could never have been made acceptable. But by and large it has been a message that officers have felt they needed to carry to the general run of members, rather than vice versa.

The second question (and it refers to both national and local levels) is to what extent has the movement been an initiative that stemmed from one political party or another? As in Lambeth, there is ample evidence of involvement of *both major parties*. It was a Conservative Home Secretary of 1957 (Henry Brooke) who so energetically set about the reform of London government. It was Sir Keith Joseph, as Conservative Minister of Housing and Local Government, who in 1964 set up the Maud Committee and who eventually also legislated the 1972 local government reorganisation. In London local government it was Tory majorities that set management reform in train when they gained many of the London boroughs in 1968 after a long period of Labour rule. On the other hand, Harold Wilson's Labour government of 1964, coming to power on the wings of its 'white heat of technology' message, made economic planning the central role of government.[45] It set up the National Economic Development Office and the 'Little Neddies' for separate industries. It created the Regional Economic Planning Councils and Boards to co-ordinate central government departments' interventions in the regions with each other and with the activities of local councils and local capital. It was a Labour administration that appointed the Royal Commission on Local Government in England. And at local level when Labour returned to many London boroughs in 1971 and 1974 they continued to develop the new structures and processes. They applied them to somewhat different ends, but nonetheless were unable or unwilling to deny their uses. The answer would seem to be that each party saw its own advantages in local government's nation-wide reorganisation and in corporate management. The Conservatives were looking for the cost-saving and efficiency that comes of tighter control, a philosophy on which they seek votes. Labour needed corporate management as an instrument primarily for more interventionist government and later, in the seventies, for drastic cuts in capital and recurrent spending.

These many forces had a cumulative effect. In 1969/70 of all county councils only 47 per cent had an overall Policy Committee, 81 per cent had a top level manager ('Principal Officer') and 44 per cent had a Management Team. In 1973 every one of the new county councils had all three. Even in the new district councils by 1973 94 per cent had a Policy Committee, 99·5 per cent had appointed a Principal Officer and 99 per cent had a Management Team.[46] Corporate management was now a fact of life in local government.

The new management in Lambeth

We should look more closely now at Lambeth Borough Council's corporate system; who was behind it; what were its apparent strengths and weaknesses from the point of view of urban management.

The Conservative leader who came to power in 1968 turned first to consultants (Urwick Orr) for advice on reshaping the architecture, planning, surveying, engineering and housing maintenance functions of the council. The result was a strong new Directorate of Development. The leader also took a decision to create a Directorate of Management Services to ensure continued advances in management. It had charge of the council's computer. He went on to replace the existing town clerk with a chief executive, who was given seven months free of practical duties to enable him to produce a complete scheme of reorganisation for the council. A lawyer by profession, the Chief Executive (CE) had been town clerk of the neighbouring borough of Southwark and was already familiar with London government problems. The scheme the CE produced and the Conservative group implemented was in all essentials that which existed four years later at the time of this case study. It reduced yet further the number of council committees (to nine) and took the 'directorate' system across the board.

We should look in particular at the housing service, because housing is a crucial function in an inner London borough. The Housing Committee in Lambeth was the 'blue chip' committee, and its chair an important political post. Lambeth was one of the first local authorities in the country to create a Comprehensive Housing Service – a characteristic adjustment being urged upon local councils at this time. The Directorate of Housing and Property Services that was thus created comprised responsibility not only for council housing but for the acquisition of private housing for the public stock, valuation, improvement grants, support for housing associations, giving mortgages to private purchasers, the administration of rent policies, research and development. The public health inspectors became part of the outfit. The overall chief officer was given the title of Director. The idea was to strengthen the housing administration by giving it more extensive, interlocking powers and, through the corporate management system of the council as a whole, to link it in strategic policy-making with the council's other main services. The Conservative council also opened the first Housing Advice Centre in Britain, with a walk-in office on the main street of Brixton.

The creation of both the Comprehensive Housing Service and the Housing Advice Centre was prompted by the appalling housing situation the Conservatives inherited in 1968. In 1967 the GLC had conducted a 4 per cent survey of housing conditions. The results of the Lambeth study were reported to the council around the time of the election. The facts shocked the new administration. Only half the dwellings in the borough could be said to be in 'good condition'. Four per cent were totally and immediately unfit. Apart from these, the survey predicted that 10 per cent of the dwellings in the borough had a life, in their present state, of no more than 7 years. Another 18 per cent had only 15 years to go. The total number of households that would have to be rehoused within 15 years, because of the poor state of housing stock, was about 40,000. Add to this an existing housing waiting list of 11,500 and the fact that there were 27,000 more households than dwellings in the borough. This gives a measure of the pressure of population on this deteriorating housing stock – and of housing on the management system of Lambeth.[47]

The Tories decided to manage the problem by a massive redevelopment programme. They announced a plan to build 14,000 units in 7 years, rehabilitate 15,000 in 15 years themselves and encourage a further 15,000 'rehabs' in the private sector in the same period. It was the task of the new comprehensive Housing Directorate to bring together the public and private resources needed for this huge effort. The new Directorate of Development had to find the land and schedule the building. The Housing Advice Centre, as it turned out, was to take pressure off Lambeth housing by exporting population. The best advice in the circumstances it could give those who came for help was to find jobs and homes in Peterborough and other new and expanding towns. The Conservative housing policy thus included social engineering as well as construction engineering.[48]

The formal map of the council as it was in 1974 is shown in Fig. 1. There was a series of nine main committees reporting to the council. Each supervised an area of work mainly carried out by one directorate under the control of a chief officer, the director. The idea, however, was that the committees should not match the directorates one-for-one, but should have responsibility for policy areas on which the work of several directorates might bear.

The crucial contribution of the Tory leadership and the Chief

Lambeth Borough Council Corporate Structure

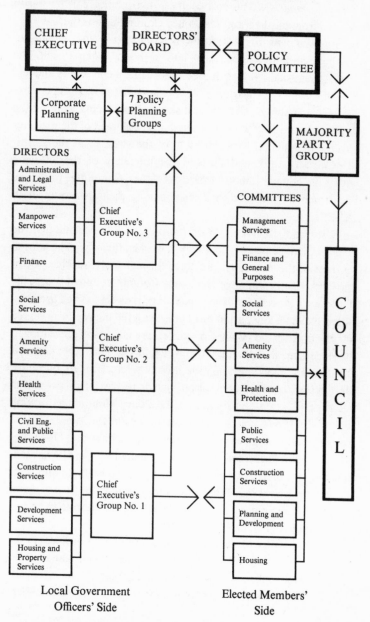

Local Government
Officers' Side

Elected Members'
Side

Executive was, however, the creation of a *Director's Board* and a *Policy Committee*. The role of these two bodies can be partly inferred from the diagram. The Policy Committee was the 'cabinet'. Its purpose was to turn formerly competitive and semi-autonomous committee chairmen into a policy-making unit. As one of them said, 'at least it meets more like a committee and less like an assembly of warlords'. It was intended to increase control by the leadership on the political side and, excluding as it did the opposition, it also of course strengthened the hand of the majority party. In Lambeth, as a reflection of the strength of the constituency party rank and file and the militancy of the left-wing within the council Labour group, the Policy Committee had three backbench members, elected from among their own number in 1974.[49]

It was the *Directors' Board*, however, that became the true heart of management in Lambeth. It worked this way. The normal business of the council is conducted through a six-weekly cycle of meetings. Each committee, the Policy Committee and of course the full council, meet in sequence once every six weeks. The Directors' Board played a key part in this cycle. As a full board it was geared into the cycle of the Policy Committee, preparing and presenting to the leadership all the material on which its decisions were based. It acted as an 'agenda group' one month before Policy Committee meetings; met a second time as an 'agenda review group' two weeks before; and again shortly before the Policy Committee meeting took place. It was not only the input to the Policy Committee that was so closely managed by the senior officers, however. Three subgroups of the Directors' Board, each chaired by the CE himself, took responsibility between them for all the committees and went through the same kind of three-meeting procedure for each of them. Any item being placed on a committee's agenda normally had to pass through one of these mini-boards.

It is possible to see the way all the threads of business in the town hall were now pulled together by the CE and his management team of senior officers. A chairman commented on the disadvantages of this corporate officer control for him as a political member.

Every report presented to a committee goes through all these processes and through the Directors' Board. We only get one report now where, before, various chief officers would have reported separately and given us their observations. One was more easily able to weigh up policy. Now they can be quite determined to get their agreed policy through and you don't know what rows there have been at director level.

This is in strong contrast to the way things used to be done, when departments and their committees carried on in more or less isolated partnership.

The council had devised for the CE's post the role that Maud and McKinsey and other outside influences were recommending and which is now found in many local authorities. He was 'pure management', trying to wean his directors, too, away from close identification with their departments, from too much attention to detail. His three main roles, as he saw them, were first to ensure that the corporate planning process worked (I shall describe later what that meant) and if necessary to design adjustments to the structure to enable it to do so. He was thus the maintenance engineer of the decision system. His second job was to chair the Directors' Board and its sub-groups, co-ordinating all departmental business and processing the information that came up to committee through these meetings. Third, he kept a watching eye on the way the directorates carried out decisions taken in Directors' Board and in Committee. The unobtrusive means by which the idea of officer-rule could be sustained as a reality was by keeping contact between officers and councillors largely to the top of the pyramid. Thus he himself saw the leader more or less every day. He fostered good working relationships between directors and chairmen. He tried to ensure that the directors worked as a team, understanding and sharing each other's points of view. This was clearly aimed at reducing the risk of a director pairing up strongly with his chairman and dominating the process in the interest of one particular function of the authority. Of course, in practice, it was difficult to prevent this happening.

The directors varied in their approach to corporate

management. Some were fully behind it. 'Decisions are taken corporately by all chief officers. We are learning more about each other's fields. I'm more aware now of other directorates. I'm more able to talk about their work – more involved,' said one director in. interview. Some, though, would boldly bypass the corporate planning system (see below) if the interests of their directorates seemed to require it. It was a continuing struggle for the corporate planners to hold the maverick Director of Development (with his statutory planning process) and the Director of Finance (with his annual rate-making process) into the corporate planning system.

Corporate management was not, for all this, the instrument of the CE and his team of directors alone. Like the Tory leader of 1968–71, the leader of the majority Labour group in 1974 was heavily involved in management. He was in his thirties; an associate member of the Chartered Insurance Institute, working in an insurance firm. He spent a good deal of his time in the council offices and sat in on many committee meetings in addition to Policy Committee (which he of course chaired), Group and full council. 'He loves politics. Even if he were losing, he'd love it,' said one of his backbenchers. His Chairman of Finance (1971–74), even younger than himself, was an advocate of management and planning and indeed later went on to take a paid job as a corporate planner in a neighbouring borough. What the leader was looking for in corporate management was, as he himself put it, 'a machine to see political objectives achieved'. He was not averse to a clear division of labour between member and officer, and between leadership and backbenchers. While he at all times consulted the majority group, and obtained their endorsement or otherwise of policies put forward and gave his backbenchers information in the shape of the Plan volumes, he did not involve them in the processes of actually making or implementing policies. 'Group wouldn't thank me for involving them in all these things,' he said. It is important to recognise, however, that many policies take their shape more from early discussions and from the way they are later carried out, than from the formal stage of decision-taking. The leader's working document was the *Management Pages*, the specialised, more detailed and partly confidential manual that accompanied the public volume of the council's *Corporate Plan* in 1974.

While the formal diagram of management gave great opportunities for control to the bureaucracy in Lambeth, there were less formal happenings, all part of this more self-conscious decision process, for which there is no part in the diagram. They tended to bring the political leadership more into the picture. For instance, when it came to thinking out what structure and what management processes the council should adopt, probably the most significant event was a couple of weekend 'think tanks' held at Tunbridge Wells soon after Labour returned to power. Here the top brass (Policy Committee, CE and Directors) met together, quite outside normal business, to thrash out principle and make plans about how to govern. In a different way, special purpose working parties, frequently used in Lambeth to analyse problems like homelessness or policy issues like family planning services, have given elected members a somewhat independent inlet to policy-making, enabling them to call at will on outside experts or on junior or middle-rank officers. 'We've discovered a way of by-passing the Directors' Board,' said a chairman. Not that working parties were felt to be democratic merely for being councillors' things. Some backbenchers felt that they were instruments of the leadership: used either to pursue a favoured line of policy and thereby present a more irrefutable case to officers, backed up by analysis; or alternatively to fob off a member or group of members with a bee-in-their-bonnet about something on which the leadership was less than enthusiastic.

It is quite possible to have a corporate management system and to carry on the normal committee cycle in a corporate style without introducing a corporate *planning* process. But corporate planning is the opportunity for applying better information, more 'intelligent' analysis and modern techniques of prediction and policy design to urban management. It is the active right hand of the new system, and Lambeth's CE when he took up his post in 1970 made sure that it was part of the package.[50] From October

1970 onwards corporate planning was supervised and promoted by a small unit under the direction of a Corporate Planning and Programming Officer. This little unit was the CE's only department.

The first product of corporate planning in Lambeth was a five-year rolling corporate plan, published as *The Community Plan* by the Conservative Leader three months before the 1971 election. It was adopted by the outgoing council on 24 March 1971 and announced to the press with a good deal of fanfare. The leader saw it, in part, as is clear from his introduction to the plan, as a document that would draw ratepayers into participation in decisions that were likely to involve them in an increased rate bill over the years. The plan was not costed in detail, nor were there adequate performance measures defined, by which its success or failure could have been evaluated by the planners. It was, as the leader of the time said, 'a comprehensive body of information to *assist* the formulation of future policies'.

A Labour opposition spokesman labelled the Conservative plan an election gimmick. Nonetheless when Labour swept back to power after this Tory interruption, they did not scrap the planning process nor did they reject the plan documents. 'One leading member said, at first,' reported the CE,[51] 'they would have to repeal it. But they found it was not so much a plan as a flexible set of policies. They found they could write their policies in and write the others out. They began to use it and found it helpful. Now they quote it to each other.' The new leader (1971–73) who had, as deputy leader of the opposition, criticised the plan so ferociously, was quick to be reconciled to it. 'His background helped,' commented an officer. 'He understood the language' (being an economics teacher).[52]

In 1974 the *Community Plan* had very much the same shape as the original Conservative Plan of 1971. It was in seven volumes, each dealing with a 'programme area'. Volume Three for instance was the planning document for the 'housing programme area'. It gave a brief statistical review of the housing situation in the borough, which was followed by three major sections on: the redevelopment and improvement programme; management of council housing; and housing advice and assistance. Under numerous sub-heads were specified *objective, need, scope of service, targets* for the coming five years, longer term *goals* – and finally various *issues* and problems were raised and discussed. The subhead 3.2.1 'Clearance of unfit areas of houses' may stand as an example. It gave criteria of fitness; the number of dwellings in the borough confirmed 'unfit', awaiting demolition and recently demolished; the number of dwellings currently being 'represented' as unfit to obtain approval for demolition. A major problem raised under 'issues' was that 'over seven hundred represented unfit houses are still occupied of which three hundred were represented over five years ago'.

Such brief outlines of position and intention were no more than a modest planning exercise yet short notes like this on each aspect of policy cumulated into a sizeable statement, and such an open account of council business had never been available to the public before corporate planning was introduced. Indeed such explicit administration was new to officers and members too.

The plan documents were the only thing that backbenchers felt they had gained by corporate planning. They felt that for the first time they had a 'map of current council activities'. That the documents were a significant addition to what backbenchers knew about the work of those committees of which they were not members, even of their own committees, as one of them admitted, was a comment on the extent to which backbenchers were cut out from the normal information flows of the council. The tightening of control in the hands of top officers and political power-holders produced by the formal design of the new management structure and the regular committee cycle was exacerbated by the way the corporate planning process was handled. It took place outside the normal cycle of committee business. Committees were too taken up with their day-to-day agendas to undertake this creative work. At the time of the case study the plan was prepared mainly by seven officer groups called Policy Planning Groups (PPGs), which met regularly throughout the year, serviced by the corporate planning staff of the CE's little unit. They corresponded in their subject matter to the terms of reference of the main spending committees, but each one pulled together representatives from all the interested services and from finance, manpower and land/building – the major resources.

The PPGs were at the outset attended by middle-rank officers from the different directorates, chaired by one of their number. The corporate planning staff found, however, that the directors, whose commitment to the Plan they needed, were not really showing enough interest in the PPGs. So they decided it would be better if the director most concerned were to chair each PPG. In this way another key role fell to the chief officer corps.

No elected members sat on these PPGs, where the Plan originated. Neither the leader nor the Chief Executive felt this to be practicable or appropriate. The CE explained that he saw 'the research and documentation for corporate planning primarily as an officer process'. Nonetheless, the work of the PPGs, work that he saw as 'research and documentation' others felt to be the fundamental plan-making activity, the phase when decisions really took shape.

The 'officer corporate planning process', a term used by the Chief Executive, was a long-term process, laying the foundations of policy and aspiring to continuity. When commenting on new policies introduced at short notice by the political leadership the CE said, 'the officer corporate planning process, which starts from the base of existing Council policies, gets overlaid sometimes by new member-level proposals'. The existence of a written plan, however, with agreed procedures for devising and revising it, reduced the likelihood of unreasonable or disruptive innovations by members. 'I like to think that the plan documents give members a greatly improved information base on which to initiate new proposals.' While they informed, however, the plan documents also implied the feasible limits to change. Ultimately, of course, the CE was able to lean on the fact that the creation of a corporate management and planning system such as this was partly enabled by and partly brought in its wake leadership by the type of councillor who talks the same language and shares the same priorities.*

These plan proposals, worked out by officers in the Policy Planning Groups, were in the early years of corporate planning introduced to members in comprehensive form in the course of a normal committee meeting: they were just an extra item on the agenda. This meant that even when the plan did surface to members' view they had only a hurried glimpse of it. The plan, a vital formulation of future intentions, tended to get lost in an agenda crowded with day to day business. It was later recognised that the time allowed for discussion was inadequate and from 1973 special meetings of some committees were arranged at which the plan was the only item on the agenda.[53]

Nonetheless, in 1974, backbenchers I spoke to did not feel very involved in corporate planning. All those who had been councillors during the previous cycle were aware of having attended or known of a committee meeting at which the plan had been discussed. But they felt on the whole that they had not been engaged in it. Indeed, one Labour backbencher said, 'It doesn't affect me. It might as well never have happened. It's a lot of waste paper.' Whatever they thought of the virtues or vices of the corporate system, the chairmen and vice-chairmen to whom I spoke, in contrast to these backbenchers, at least felt they had played some part in the planning cycle, even if too little and too late.

Many Labour backbenchers felt obscurely that corporate planning was increasing rather than diminishing the gulf between themselves and the leader and powerful chairmen of committee, and that it was doing nothing to enhance the interaction (except at the highest level) between councillors and officers. 'Elected members should have more say in the decisions made (ostensibly) by Lambeth councillors. At the moment, most decisions are taken by paid officials, agreed to readily by the clique which in effect

---

* The CE was dissatisfied with the above discussion of elected members' part in corporate planning and asked me to add that 'there was a continual member-level influence on the process both from council and committee decisions and informally'.

controls the Labour group, and then generally passed by councillors too inert or disinterested to either question or complain.' And again, 'most members haven't got the time or energy to get to grips with these things. You get a director who's a ball of fire, and he can run away with it.'

Add to this set of circumstances the fact that, not only here in Lambeth but in many local authorities, councillors who are not accustomed, by their experience, to paper work and analytical reading and a quick grasp of financial accounts, seldom get the opportunity to hold office. In a local authority with a big budget and modernised management system the tendency must be for them to remain backbenchers. Manual workers and low-paid non-manual workers are thus doubly excluded. They are excluded from office, and as backbenchers they tend to be excluded from any creative part in the decision-process.

The corporate planning staff themselves were anxious about the effect on ordinary members of corporate management. They were trying to be tacticians of democracy. They wanted to overcome the situation in which the councillor is a mere ghost in the corridor, padding round the town hall after dark, when the officers whose manor it really is have gone home. The more general theory of corporate management, too, presses the need for corporate management to recognise the political rights and uses of the ordinary councillor.[54] But it was among the contradictions of urban management that such a tendency was impossible to reconcile with the priorities of tighter control.

In other respects Lambeth council was reflecting quite closely the proposals that had emanated from central government, from INLOGOV, and from corporate management literature as a whole during the period of its creation. The vertical pyramid of control had grown taller and thinner. Directorate work was horizontally integrated in the Directors' Board. Whereas in the old days the majority group and the council itself had been a place where the affairs of many committees had been aired, in front of backbenchers and of the public, now, though Group was still technically sovereign, opinions were being formed and decisions hardened in Policy Committee. The council meeting had long become, in the words of members, 'a set piece, a farce, a public relations show'. More important still, behind all the activity of Group, committees and council stood the considerable organisation of officers. 'The real power in the town hall lies with the officers. It always has and it always will.'

Any evaluation of corporate management has to be made from two points of view simultaneously. It has to be evaluated on its own terms – because only by recognising its successes and failures from the point of view of the managers does it become possible to understand their reactions and the further development of their management systems. But it also has to be evaluated from a working-class point of view, that of ordinary people living or working in the borough.

From the council's point of view, corporate management in Lambeth had three main defects – recognised by the corporate planners and apparent also in performance. First, being an affair mainly of top-level management, it was unable to have much impact on putting the council's corporately-decided plans and policies *into effect*. Second, for the same reason, it did little to enhance contact between the council and local people and organisations and so was unable to develop the amount of up-to-date and accurate information that was needed about the governed population. Third, by strengthening the hand of senior officers and, secondarily, of the political leadership, it made local government appear even less 'democratic' than before, and so diminished the legitimacy it needed if authority was to be unquestioned. The responses of the management system to these weaknesses in Lambeth and in local government in Britain more generally are discussed in Chapters 4 and 5.

In evaluating the advantages and disadvantages of corporate management in local government for ordinary working people again we have to take two viewpoints. First, that of workers on the council payroll. Second that of the local electorate, the 'consumers' of council services in the local population.

As would be expected, the strengthening of management in the town hall had had a constraining effect on council workers.

One aspect of corporate management in Lambeth was greatly to increase investment in the personnel management function. 'The establishment side has grown from a couple of dozen to more than a hundred people in just a few years,' reported the NALGO Action Group[55] secretary in Lambeth. 'Every directorate now has its own personnel people. You can't turn round for them.'

The resources of which Lambeth was so short were finance, land and manpower. Land and money were more or less constant constraints, more or less outside the council's power, from one day to the next, to alter. The remaining resource was of course people, the only one that was marginally flexible, that could be recruited, dismissed, trained, made more productive. While the number of manual staff on the council's payroll was more or less constant between 1967 and 1974, standing at 3,600, the number of office staff doubled, going from 1,800 to 3,600 in this period. The work of the directorate concerned with 'establishment' therefore was of some significance.[56] Its work was manpower planning. Along with the tasks of training, staff development and employee relations it was responsible for job evaluation and had reviewed and evaluated some two thousand office worker[57] posts in the year 1973–74. The unit concerned with productivity services had a staff of thirty-six. They were responsible for work study, 'ensuring that, in those services employing manual operatives, optimum rewards commensurate with improved levels of productivity are achieved and maintained'. Thirteen work study schemes were being implemented, covering 1,400 operatives in housing maintenance, highways maintenance, sewers maintenance and construction, street lighting, cemeteries, transport and plant maintenance. Further work study schemes were planned on conversion and new building work, depot labourers, street sweeping, bulk container steam cleaning, street market cleaning, laundries and public conveniences, housing caretakers and cleansing services, portering services, catering and baths. A parallel exercise was in hand on the office side, involving studies among others on the efficiency of internal messenger services, typing services and social work area-office practices. The pressure on productivity and conditions of work for the council's employees had thus considerably increased in the period that corporate management was introduced.

The effect of corporate management on the local population outside the town hall is less clear-cut. Rational, intelligent and forward-looking management is an undeniably good value in any organisation to those whose interests that organisation serves. Management takes a form specific to an organisation and it cannot be evaluated without also evaluating the purposes of the organisation and its relationship to others around it. In the case of local government it is impossible to assess the effect of the new management ways on the local working class without understanding much more about the function of local government, the place it has in the structure of state and its relationship with business interests.

For instance, corporate management may well, as it grows more experienced, result in better value for money spent in terms of services. Whether this is a total or a partial gain for the recipient of those services will depend on the answers to yet other questions. Who is really paying for the services? (who is the 'ratepayer', where do central government grants to local councils originate?) Who needs the services? (is it ourselves only, or our employers too?) Who controls their administration? (ourselves or the authorities?)

Conversely, corporate management as we've seen tends to exclude the ordinary elected councillor from effective decision making. Much of the foregoing account has reflected the consciousness of some councillors and officers of certain 'anti-democratic' tendencies in corporate management. This is clearly bad for the representation of working class interests. But to see it therefore as wholly good for those who represent other class interests is to ignore the complexity of the part played by local electoral democracy and the Labour Party in such a place as Lambeth today. This anticipates the discussion of following chapters, where it will become clear that attempts to correct the anti-democratic shortcomings of corporate management by means of 'the community approach' have to be seen themselves as *management* initiatives.

We can get little further in understanding the significance of corporate management, or of community development, without a more detailed picture of local government, its place in the society and economy we live in and the pressures to which it responds.

2. Local government as local state

We need a view of local government that explains the connections thrown up in this story of corporate management, the working connections between central government and local government, local councils and other state authorities at local level, connections between the world of government and the world of business. We need an analysis that sets local government in the context of the real economic situation of the period in which we live and asks: what is its job? Such an approach involves stepping outside the conventional frame of reference and seeing local government, our old red-brick town hall, for what it really also is: a key part of the state in capitalist society. Such a step doesn't come easily. We have been taught to think of local government as a kind of humane official charity, a service that looks after us 'from the cradle to the grave', protects us from the misfortunes of life, hardships such as poverty and homelessness that fall on us by fate – or are perhaps even our own fault. If the town hall doesn't seem to work in our interest we put it down to 'inefficiency' or 'red tape'. It is by no means obvious that a local council is part of a structure which *as a whole and in the long term* has other interests to serve than our own.

There is no ready-made theory of local government. It is necessary to piece together a number of concepts about the state as a whole and draw conclusions from them for local government. There are three fundamental ideas in the early writings of Marx on which later work has built. They are crucial for any real understanding of the role of local government. The first of these is that the state can only be understood by looking at the way wealth is produced in a particular society. It is specific to the mode of production.

> The social structure and the state are continually evolving out of the
> life process of definite individuals, but of individuals, not as they
> appear in their own or other people's imagination, but as they really
> are, i.e. as they operate, produce materially and hence as they work
> under definite material limits, presuppositions and conditions,
> independent of their will.[1]

We cannot think of the state in the abstract — it is always specific to
a historical time and place. In reaching an understanding of the
local state in Britain today, therefore, we should be clear that this is
to say little about the nature of the local state arising from
different modes of production.[2]

The second basic idea is that the state in capitalism is an
instrument of class domination, that in the modern state the
bourgeoisie, the dominant class who own capital and employ
workers, holds political sway.[3] As such, the state is at the heart of
the perennial struggle between the bourgeoisie and those it exploits
— the working class. Indeed it exists because of this struggle,
because the society has become entangled in an insoluble contradiction with itself and is irreconcilably divided.[4] In looking at the
state as we know it, then, even our own London borough local
state, we cannot avoid considering local and national class
interests.

The third theme in the original marxist concept of the state is
that its characteristic function is repression: its main role is to keep
the working class in its place and to set things up, with forceful
sanctions, in such a way that capital itself, business interests as a
whole, normally survive and prosper. The state in this view is seen
as above all being the armed forces, the police, the judges and
courts of law.

We should look in more detail at these last two ideas, the
relationship of the state to class, and the changing role of the state.
They have been amplified by recent work, some of which can help
the understanding of local government. This contemporary theory,
though, in no way weakens the identification of the state with the
economic base of society, nor as the agent of capital. What it does
is to increase the scope of the services the state is seen as

performing for capital and explain in more detail how it performs them. In looking at these two developments of marxist theory we can see too how they make sense of changes in local government and its management system.

Class and state: the hidden links

To take the first question first: how do such relationships between class and state find expression in a place like Lambeth? One way of describing the population of Lambeth is in terms of their type of occupation. This distribution is given in the table which shows, clustering in the north and central wards of the

Lambeth's Population Described by the Occupations of its Male Workers[5]

	North Lambeth %	Central Lambeth %	South Lambeth %
Group A: employers and managers, professional workers, etc.	8·5	12·0	20·0
Group B: foremen and supervisors, etc.	33·0	31·0	30·0
Group C: non-manual, clerical, sales, etc.	20·5	25·0	29·0
Group D: unskilled manual workers, etc.	38·0	32·0	21·0
Total male workers	100·0	100·0	100·0

borough, a population mainly of relatively poor people, semi-skilled or unskilled workers or unemployed; and in the more salubrious southern wards a population that is relatively better-off, with more skilled manual, professional and managerial people. The territorial boundary is not as distinct, of course, as this summary implies. The popular view, and one which seems to be shared by the Conservative and Labour councillors in Lambeth, is that such statistical distributions demonstrate a borough divided into a middle class and a working class who are in competition with each other over the rate burden and for the resources of which the council disposes. Indeed the council seems sometimes to foment differences between different groups of residents for the purposes of control. False categories are played off against each other, the 'ratepayer' against 'the council tenant', 'council tenant' against 'homeless' or 'squatter'. This definition of relatively minor differences of interest obscures a much more fundamental class division that operates in Lambeth – one which the authorities are at pains *not* to invoke. This is the division between this urban population as a whole and the class that owns capital in Lambeth, controls its land and employs its workers, collects both rents from the tenants and interest on the mortgages taken out by owner-occupiers. Seen this way, it is laughable to suppose that the owner-occupiers of Norwood or Streatham in the south, taken as a category, are the class enemy of the council tenants of Vassall and Angell wards in the north. With their semi-detached properties and a couple of thousand pounds invested through a unit trust, many are as vulnerable to the bankers, brokers and building societies as tenants are to landlords. They may sometimes act competitively with the poorer working class, they may vote Tory. But the real dominant class of Lambeth are infinitely more powerful than this, and are in the main invisible.*

---

* A useful discussion of class occurs in a recent article by E. Olin Wright:

'Some marxists have argued that only productive manual workers should be considered part of the proletariat. Others have argued that the working class includes low-level, routinized white-collar employees as well. Still others have argued that virtually all wage-labourers should be considered part of the working class. . . . It matters a great deal for our understanding of class struggle and social change exactly how classes are conceptualized and which categories of social positions are placed in which classes.'

Wright argues that employees in 'unproductive' jobs, mental labour, supervisory labour and other doubtful categories must be seen as occupying objectively contradictory locations between classes. The more contradictory is a position within social relations of production, the more political and ideological relations can influence its objective position within class relations.

In this study I adopt a similarly inclusive definition of working class. For instance I include local state workers, except for senior officers associated with policy-making. I would argue that if their subjective inclination and their political practice identifies them as workers there is no objective constraint to their inclusion. Likewise I hold it inappropriate

Lambeth is mainly a dormitory area. Many manufacturing firms have moved away. We shall see why and with what effect in Chapter 3. Those that remain are on the whole the smaller and less competitive firms. This face of the local bourgeoisie seems relatively aged and feeble. The class forces that work more powerfully on Lambeth's population are the shareholders and directors of commercial firms in the City of Westminster that employ Lambeth's commuters, the finance companies in the City of London and abroad from whom the council borrows a fair proportion of its massive loan, and whose operations lie behind so many movements of capital in the borough. The property dealers and speculators that own and develop Lambeth's land; shareholders of building companies that find their business in its housing programmes; professionals in the big firms of estate agents, soliticors and quantity surveyors that make a livelihood out of these processes – few of these live in the borough, but they are its dominant class nonetheless.

If we have to dissolve the borough boundary to see the real class divisions that exist there, we have to do the same in order to see the real 'local' authorities. It is clearly not the council alone that represents the state at local level. The powerful business interests scarcely notice a local council. Deals that matter most to them, over taxation and employment policy, grants and controls, are deals done with Westminster and Whitehall. The council is only a small part of a large state structure.

The state nationally has its headquarters in London but it comprises nationwide and permanent institutions. The armed forces, the judiciary, and the police are found in local barracks, courts of law and police stations. In the same way central

---

to see owner-occupiers, as a category, as bourgeois. Successive governments have used owner-occupation purposefully as an inducement to workers to identify with bourgeois values. I reserve the term bourgeoisie for those who own substantial capital and who profit from the surplus value created by labour; plus those professionals, managers, etc., who identify with and further this process. See further discussion in Chapter 3. (E. Olin Wright, 'Class Boundaries in Advanced Capitalist Societies', *New Left Review*, no. 98, July–August 1976.)

government departments dealing with education, housing and health, while they may have large offices in London SW1, carry out their work in and through schools and education offices; housing estates and local housing departments; hospitals and local health authorities. These are often technically the responsibility of a local council or other local or regional authority. Their officials nonetheless are state employees. Certain services are administered locally direct by the central state – one such is social security, another is the post office. Together these local agencies make up the state at local level.

It is widely believed that local government is in some way constitutionally independent of central government. Herein lies the source of the confusion, for example, over the question of whether or not we are seeing a 'decline in local democracy'. Central government has more and more of a say in local government affairs. But if local councils' responsibilities and activities and expenditure are continually increasing, as they have done for many decades, how can it be that we are witnessing a decline in local government, which many officers and councillors in local government believe to be so? The misapprehension lies in the belief that local councils spring from some ancient right of grassroots self-government. This is not the case. They are, and under capitalism have always been, subject to central government. Lord Redcliffe-Maud, probably the most authoritative voice on local government in Britain and chairman of three major commissions, insists:

> Local government in modern England is the creation of Parliament
> . . . the organs of local government today take all their important
> characteristics from Acts of Parliament. Further, Parliament has
> not been content merely to give them powers and a set of bounds
> beyond which they may not pass: in some cases it has also
> positively prescribed what they must do. Local authorities are thus
> obliged to provide certain services and allowed to provide others.
> They can do practically nothing else which costs money.[6]

Thus local authorities, including local health, water and transport authorities as well as local education, housing and planning authorities, are aspects of the national state and share its work.

When I refer to Lambeth Borough Council as 'local state' it is to say neither that it is something distinct from 'national state', nor that it alone represents the state locally. It is to indicate that it is part of a whole.

As to the relations between state and capital, it should not be surprising that it is difficult to see direct and immediate connections. The dominant class operating upon Lambeth, as anywhere, is divided into fractions with somewhat different interests. Although the prospects of all of them objectively depend in the long run on the health and growth of the capitalist system, big city finance may well have different short-run interests, when it comes to developments in Lambeth, to those, say, of local manufacturing industry. The state can hardly play to so many marginally different interests the simple role of 'secretariat'. The several 'fractions' of capital cannot alone overcome their economic differences. Besides, the militancy of the working class aggravates their problems. So the capitalist state looks after the bourgeoisie's interests as a whole and sets up and maintains the cultural and political domination of the working class that capitalism as a whole needs if it is to continue.[7]

In order to do its work of organising the dominant classes and politically disorganising the working class, the state keeps a certain distance from any one bourgeois fraction.[8] It does not directly or continuously represent, for instance, Times Furnishing of Brixton Road, Imperial Chemical Industries or the International Monetary Fund. It is not entirely in the pocket of the products of Marlborough and Eton; or of the legal profession or the top military. It could not do its work for capital if it were. An example of this relative autonomy of the state was the transfer of corporate management from capitalist enterprise to local government – the world of business did not intervene directly; the routes taken by the new management principles were various and indirect.

In spite of its multiplicity, however, the state preserves a basic unity. All its parts work *fundamentally* as one. In the corporate management movement we saw how central government, local government, the universities and research institutes, the professional associations and the political parties worked together, achieving an effective change in a short time. In Lambeth the homeless are finding, likewise, that the police, the electricity board, the gas corporation, the social security and the local council reveal a practical unity in their efforts to put an end to squatting. This detached integrity is important at an ideological level too because it helps to perpetuate the idea that the state does not represent the particular interest of capital but the general interest, the general will, the political unity of 'the people and nation', bosses and workers alike.

Nominally in control of the permanent structure of the state is a changeable component: the elected bodies. They comprise both Parliament and the many elected local councils.

The conventional view of electoral representative government takes two forms. For those who believe that the nation is basically united in its interests, the democratic process exists to give form to this consensus. For those who take the liberal view that uncontrolled *laissez-faire* has detrimental effects on ordinary people, the democratic process exists to keep a check on capital's excesses, looking for fair solutions. But if the state is, as the materialist view supposes, an expression of dominant class interests in capitalism, existing specifically to perpetuate a class system, neither of these conventional views holds water. What part then do elections and a political party system play?

One of the contradictions of capitalism is the necessity of maintaining a class system while at the same time weaning the working class away from class identification that could lead to class militancy. Electoral democracy, with its set of political parties, helps in this situation in that it appears, to those who insist on thinking in class terms, to enable adequate representation of the working class. Yet it also contrives to appear classless in a classless society.

The engagement of a social-democratic party 'of the working class' in such a system is an important mechanism for legitimating state power, for securing the co-operation of working class leaders, channelling political action into an institutional mould. It ensures a cutting-off of the political activity of the working class from its economic power and organisation on the shop floor of industry. Ralph Miliband has documented the history of the young, idealist Labour Party of the first two decades of this century. The members of parliament that the labour movement had hoped would put working class interests on the agenda of the House of Commons were manipulated and co-opted into a 'national interest'.[9] Miliband chronicles many instances in which the Labour Party leadership was led to forfeit working class interests in their concern 'to reassure the dominant classes and the business elites as to their intentions, to stress that they conceived their task in "national" and not in "class" terms, to insist that their assumption of office held no threat to business.'[10] We should not be surprised, then, when a Labour group on a local council espouse the principles of corporate planning and urban management, as they did in Lambeth. We should be surprised if they did not. In their turn, as Miliband showed, the left-wing radicals of the Labour Party are transformed as they step into the Party's national leadership.[11] Likewise we should not expect the handful of militant leftwing backbenchers in the Lambeth Labour Group to attain high office, or having attained it, to keep it unless they modify their former political stance.

The process of parliament and of local councils serves to institutionalise class contest and to project a colourless version of the fundamental struggle that takes place elsewhere. The state has, besides, developed certain defences against the incursions of working class interests via parliament and councils.[12] As the working class won the vote in the reform acts of the late nineteenth and early twentieth centuries and came to be in a position to send their representatives to Westminster, the power of Parliament gradually receded into the civil service and to the Cabinet, more amenable to the permanent interests of the state. Likewise, in Lambeth and other local authorities power long ago shifted from the Council Chamber to committee and thence, with the intro- duction of corporate management, to the top-level Policy Committee. Leftwing backbenchers are left with the trappings of power – the real thing lies with the leadership, those who are ready to adopt the proper behaviour of urban managers. And a Labour leadership showing any tendency to socialist zeal is quickly curbed by the decision-making power of senior permanent officials.

The story of Clay Cross provides a recent illustration of these mechanisms at work. The militant Labour councillors of Clay Cross, a small coal-mining town in Derbyshire, refused to implement the Conservative Housing Finance Act 1971, which would have required them to raise the rents of their council tenants. At first they were only one among many Labour-controlled councils to stand out against the Act. One by one, however, the others capitulated until finally it was only Clay Cross councillors who stood firm against the threat of personal bankruptcy. (The state has the power to 'surcharge' elected members personally for council expenditure that is outside the bounds sanctioned by government.) The working class of Clay Cross were for a brief period fully represented by their 'representative' council – the class struggle had been extended from the coalfield to the council chamber. But the conditions for such an achievement in local electoral democracy are rare and, when they occur, short-lived. A Housing Commissioner was despatched to Clay Cross by central government to bring the Labour group to heel and to administer housing directly. The District Auditor was sent in to assess the cost of the councillors' revolt. The members were taken to court and the Labour Party nationally failed to stand by its local militants. By a neat, but not altogether fortuitous, turn of fate, the local government reorganisation following the 1972 Act, implemented some months later, wiped the local authority of Clay Cross from the map of government.[13]

This tendency in parliamentary democracies clearly doesn't lead to an absolute condition of working class impotence, nor is the struggle all sham for being institutionalised. In Clay Cross it was real enough. The play within the structure of the state, needed to enable the co-ordination of the interests of a divided dominant class, also affords opportunities for working class militancy to win concessions. The stance of the state at any one time will depend in part on the pressures brought to bear by the working class. The situation is dynamic: the state is not tightly in control of circumstance but is continually coping with a changing balance of power. Though capital and the state *structure* the situation of struggle, they by no means always have the initiative. This gives meaning to the several stages of the introduction of the new management measures into local authorities, as we shall see.

Welfare state: serving or servicing?

To move now to the second question, that of the practical job of the state in modern capitalism. Recent history, the growth of a 'mixed economy' and of a welfare state, has made it clear beyond all doubt that the state has an economic as well as a purely repressive role in society. This is not to deny that the state uses force for political ends – Northern Ireland is a contemporary reminder. Nor that it is indifferent to property rights – witness the current proposals for tightening the law of conspiracy and trespass. These roles remain as crucial to capital as ever. But, because of changes in capitalism, it has been forced to intervene increasingly in the economic sphere.

The state's primary role is continually *to reproduce the conditions within which capitalist accumulation can take place.* In many of its economic interventions it does this more or less directly. It attempts to control the economy and its business cycles, deflating, reflating and so on. It provides cheap utilities (power, communications, etc.) that help national industry to compete with foreign capital. In response to a decline in manufacturing industry the state has recently taken on yet more direct intervention, investing capital in ailing firms, affording grant-aid and tax relief to more. 'Planning agreements' introduced by the Industry Act 1975 are a further step: an attempt to integrate company development with state economic planning. What is sought (in the words of Lord Ryder, the ex-chairman of Reed International and current chairman of the government's National Enterprise Board), is a 'co-operative partnership with industry'.[14]

The term 'mixed economy' is often used to describe the situation that results from the state's direct intervention in economic matters, implying a half-socialist hybrid. This is misleading. Nationalised enterprises such as road, rail, electricity and gas undertakings are more significant to industry in assuring cheap basic utilities than they are to the worker – who finds himself in an unchanged wage relationship within them. They may be termed 'mixed economy' but 'whatever ingenious euphemism may be invented for them, these are still in all essentials and despite the transformations which they have undergone, authentically capitalist societies'.[15]

So the state intervenes directly and increasingly in productive aspects of the capitalist economy – it exhorts, regulates, controls, buys and invests. Typically this is the role of the central state, of Westminster and Whitehall. But local authorities too are increasingly involved directly in the affairs of capital. A number of recent studies have traced the connections between local councils and local business.[16] The Community Land Act 1975, obliging councils to buy and manage redevelopment land, will involve an urban council such as Lambeth more deeply with property and finance capital; many have already tried out profit-sharing schemes, and councils are increasingly interested in investing share capital in local firms.[17]

The diagram opposite shows the state role of 'contributing to capitalist production' and places it adjacent to another function, called 'contributing to capitalist REPRODUCTION'. This reproduction role we have to look at more closely, because it is in this that most of the activities of local councils, certainly those we think of as most typically town hall business, can be found. To understand management developments like corporate planning and community development in local authorities it is necessary to understand *what it is* that local government is trying to manage.

The capitalist system is based upon production, what goes on in the mines, factories, farms and building sites. But naturally, if production is to continue indefinitely, it also depends on renewing,

Securing conditions favourable to
capital accumulation

Contributing to capitalist reproduction

Reproducing the labour force

Reproducing the relations of production

Ideology

Repression

Contributing to capitalist production

Functions of the State in Capitalism

extending and modernising all the time the 'general conditions' and means of production. Capitalist societies must therefore have mechanisms for REPRODUCING themselves.[18] Specifically, two things must be reproduced. First, the productive *forces*. Second, the existing *relations* of production.

Renewing productive forces means, at one level, that capital, machinery, raw materials, buidings and so on must be continually forthcoming. Even in this limited respect it is easy to see that one firm alone cannot provide for its future in this way. One company exists in a whole linked structure. The machinery it needs for its processes is the manufactured product of a second firm. The steel for that machinery originates in a third. A sure supply of raw materials and growing export markets depends on external relations between nations. Nothing less than a system is needed.

At another level, though, there is *labour power* to reproduce as well: the capacity of men and women to work is the most important productive force. This process of reproducing labour power goes on mainly outside the firm. It occurs on the whole by giving people wages so that they can do it for themselves, buy their own food and housing and pay for their transport to work. But capital needs labour that is skilled and appropriate to the job, and the type and level of labour changes continually. It is no use reproducing the labour of the 1930s for the industry of the 1970s. The state therefore takes steps, on behalf of the capitalist class collectively, to do the job of *extended reproduction*: to plan for and provide education, housing, health and social services for the country as a whole.

The role of the state in reproducing the labour force existed from the earliest days of capitalism. The factory system called for state intervention in such matters as conditions and hours of child and female labour. The capitalist system could not go on indefinitely using up several generations of labour in the space of one.[19] The state also had to intervene quite early on in regulating the condition of housing and later in actually providing working class dwellings. It was already in the nineteenth century involved in the provision of basic free education.

But it is in this century that the state's responsibility for the reproduction of the labour force has increased dramatically. National insurance was introduced before the first world war. The share of council building in all house building increased rapidly in the twenties and thirties. And after the second world war the state's education system was rationalised and extended in the 1944 Education Act; a National Health Service was set up; and the national insurance scheme was greatly extended. As the country recovered from the war a massive urban reconstruction and public housing programme was set in motion. Local councils were, in the main, the agencies made responsible for this extended task.

In looking at the local state management system in this book we are at the heart of the contradictions intrinsic to the local state. There is no way therefore we can evade confronting these basic contradictions fully now, as they apply to capitalist reproduction. These services through which the state plays its part in reproducing the labour force are also services won by the working class. Years of militancy and negotiation lie behind council housing and the National Health Service. Though the capitalist mode of production may perpetuate the exploitation of the working class, workers nevertheless have to live within it. They can only build up the strength they need to challenge capitalism as a system by fighting for and winning material concessions and democratic freedoms here and now. In this respect the welfare state was a *real* gain for the working class. Nonetheless these services are not *total* gains, because to the state and capital they are not *total* losses. As the working class has an interest in receiving services, so capital has an interest in seeing them serviced. Not only does capital need efficient and appropriate labour, it also needs to disarm working class discontent that might otherwise disrupt society. The level of public expenditure is, however, always a crucial question for the capitalist economy as a whole. The struggle thus takes place over levels of provision and over the amount of control over provision given to the consumer.

The point that it is important to establish is this. The fact that we need services in no way nullifies the fact that capitalism needs us reproduced, just as the fact that we need a job and a wage in no way invalidates the truth that capitalism needs to exploit our labour power. In the account that follows of new developments in the local state we should, in the same way, not expect to see clear cut gains or losses for either class, but a jousting for initiative in an ever-developing situation of contradiction.

Returning to the second aspect of reproduction, if capitalism is to survive, each succeeding generation of workers must stay in an appropriate relationship to capital: the *relations* of production must be reproduced. Workers must not step outside the relation of the wage, the relation of property, the relation of authority. So 'reproducing capitalist relations' means reproducing the class system, ownership, above all reproducing a *frame of mind*.[20] Extended reproduction, in this context, calls to mind that as capital develops and its contradictions and crises develop too, so the relations of production have to shift dynamically also. This is a continual challenge and struggle for the dominant classes. Take one specially important relation, that of the local population to its local authority. In the recent official measures known as 'participation' and community development (discussed more fully in Chapters 4 and 5) we are witnessing the extended reproduction of this particular capitalist relation.

The job of reproducing capitalist relations is done partly by actual repression and coercion. The political nature of the police in Britain is becoming more clearly recognised.[21] Nor should we underestimate the repressiveness of many agencies that appear to have only welfare functions. The benefits system is structured to induce labour discipline. Social security and the dole, with the weekly 'signing on' requirement, closely restrict the mobility and freedom of claimants. The 'cohabitation' rule ensures that a man living with a woman takes on the responsibility for maintaining her children. This rule promotes marriage, it polices the morality of women and imposes the officially-determined share-out between state and family of responsibility for the support of children. Among those on the local payroll, school attendance officers and, less overtly, teachers and social workers are asked to regulate and control behaviour. Much more typically, however, in Britain today, reproducing capitalist relations is carried out not by repression but by ideology – by inculcating a view of the world to bring about consent.

This idea makes sense to those of us who work in or struggle against or depend upon local government in Britain. It is clear to us that Lambeth council is not simply a repressive apparatus. Indeed in some ways it would be simpler (though less comfortable) if it were, because we would see more clearly what was happening to us. Instead, reproducing capitalist relations is more and more a cultural affair. It means school, social work, electoral politics. Where fascism uses force, liberal-democracy uses cultural persuasion. As Antonio Gramsci wrote fifty years ago from an Italian prison the formal apparatus of the state is only an advance trench. Behind it lies a robust chain of fortresses – which we think of very often as unofficial, private things.[22] Ideology is particularly effective in the way it permeates many apparently private and independent domains such as the family and the media. All can be enlisted this way in the defence of the capitalist mode of production and thereby the state is massively expanded.

Historically it was the church and the family that were the most important ideological extensions of the state. The church taught obedience, brotherly love, it blessed the meek and encouraged people to turn the other cheek – no recipe for militancy at work or in politics. And the family was the place where the child was inculcated with Christian virtues. Now we have many state and so-called 'private' institutions doing the original job of the church and sharing that of the family. We have a complex set of organisations embodying a single assumption: that the existing mode of production and the system of relations that goes with it are the best and only conceivable ones for us, facts of life and laws of nature. In them we create our 'common sense' and 'know' that unfairness, inequality, poverty, homelessness or failures of justice in Britain today are merely errors in the system, errors that good intentions and good management could put right. The totalitarian experiences of twentieth-century Russia and Eastern Europe 'prove' that the overthrow of capitalism must mean the end of freedom. Democracy is ranged alongside capitalism; oppression is paired with socialism: two sets of natural twins. The working class, through bourgeois culture, is offered bourgeois values without bourgeois powers. 'The bourgeoisie poses itself as an organism in continuous movement, capable of absorbing the entire society, assimilating it to its own cultural and economic level. The entire function of the state has been transformed; the state has become an "educator".'[23]

Local state: family partnership

A local authority such as Lambeth Borough Council is deeply involved in reproducing the local labour force. Though it is not, itself, an all-purpose authority it nonetheless runs housing and social services, leisure and recreation facilities. It pays a higher authority (the Greater London Council) to educate its children; the Metropolitan Police to control them; and it collaborates with the Area Health Authority to keep them fit. The state at local level is, naturally enough, that aspect of the state as a whole that specialises in the relationship with the individual. 'Local government' is a face-to-face affair. The rent officer, the social worker, the school teacher – these represent the government to the man, woman and child in the 'client' population. Normally, however, and by preference, the state deals not with individuals but with *families*. More often than not it deals with the *woman* of the family. Who answers the door when the social worker calls? who talks to the head teacher about the truant child? who runs down to the rent office? the woman, wife and mother.

Why the family and why the woman? Because the primary responsibility for capitalist reproduction, regardless of the growing intervention of the state, remains that of the family. 'The costs of reproduction borne by the state would be infinitely greater, both if adequate socialised care were provided for all the dependants, both children and others, that have remained women's responsibility within the family and if women were to receive equal state benefits in their own right.'[24] The state is dominant in the enterprise, but it cannot do without the family.

Though the church may have lost nearly all its role to the state in this century and the last, the family still has important functions in reproducing capitalism. We should hardly be surprised by the strong contemporary link between the local state and the family. Engels a century ago showed how the two developed over long historical periods side by side in continual interaction.[25] Recently, the women's movement has taken the analysis further by recognising and arguing for greater emphasis of the concept of 'capitalist reproduction' in marxist economics. Mariarosa Dalla Costa in 1971 pointed out the inadequacy of the traditional marxist definition of the housewife's role.[26] Marxist theory had always supposed that when women remained outside social production, that is outside the paid workforce, they were performing not labour but *work*. Domestic work created use-value, benefiting the individual and the family but having no relevance to capital. Dalla Costa argued that women don't have to go out to work to be working for the capitalist system – they may not be 'producing' tangible goods in a factory but they are 'reproducing' no less tangible workers. By maintaining the worker (and the child who is learning to be worker) the housewife, unpaid by the worker's boss, yet turns out the man each morning ready for the job, fed, clothes mended, sexually serviced, cocooned by the woman's caring against the most severe of the frustrations of wage work.

'Domestic work produces not merely use values but is essential to the production of surplus value. . . . What we wish to make clear is that by the non-payment of a wage when we are producing in a capitalistically organised world, the figure of the boss is concealed behind that of the husband.' Recognising that housewives contribute directly to capitalist reproduction and hence indirectly to capitalist production, need imply neither that housework is 'productive labour' in the marxist sense nor that an appropriate demand is for a 'wage' for this work. The insight is more important for the possibilities it opens up for women's awareness of their own domestic situation, the relationship between their work at home and their own and their husband's work outside the home, and between themselves and the state through services addressed to the family, such as education, health, social work and housing. It reveals more clearly than before that 'the family' is a working part of the capitalist mode of production.

A consequence of this understanding of the economic role of the family is a recognition that if family relations are not to be capitalist relations, then a conscious struggle over the practice of family life has to take place. The traditional family performs an ideological service for capital. A conventional sociological view of the family expresses this clearly (and endorses it warmly): 'it impels the individual not only to identify with the family group and so uphold its standards, but it also exerts pressures on its members to conform to the norms, laws, mores and folkways of the wider community of which it forms a part.'[27] Within the family, often for reasons of fear, the very real anxieties of parents for their children in a bigger and more hostile world outside, the young are taught to live within the conventions, to be obedient to adult authority. Home and school combine to create acceptance of a way of life. Above all, the child is 'ascribed a social class' through the family into which it is born long before it acquires an objective relationship to capital through employment.[28] We saw the dialectical nature of the welfare state representing both gains and losses to each class simultaneously. The same is of course true of the family. We need it; and our need can be turned to our disadvantage. The state needs it – but this very need can be turned against the state. A child whose family life places her or him in the working class may not merely grow up to *work* as a worker but grow up to recognise and act upon her or his class interests. Much depends on the ideology and practice of those who live together and rear children.

Contemporary developments of capitalism and the welfare state, far from reducing the dependence of mother and wife within the family, have leaned on it.[29] In his report of 1942, the foundation stone of the welfare state, William Beveridge explicitly recognised capital's need of family and housewife.

In any measure of social policy in which regard is had to facts, the great majority of married women must be regarded as occupied on work which is vital though unpaid, without which their husbands could not do their paid work and without which the nation could not continue. . . . Mothers have vital work to do in ensuring the adequate continuance of the British Race and of British Ideals in the world.[30]

Changes in the economy, notably the period of full employment following the second world war, resulted in a huge increase in the number of married women in paid work outside the home. Meanwhile the welfare state raised working class living standards but did nothing to change the private nature of domestic work. So the combined result has been many more women than before working a double shift, one shift outside the home and another inside. The welfare services besides led to a more intrusive state supervision of the family.

Already in the 1930s Eleanor Rathbone noted the increased state supervision of mothers in the home. She pointed out that at any time health visitors, school inspectors or rent collectors could drop in unannounced, putting pressure on the mother to improve the quality of labour power she produced and holding legal sanctions against her if she failed to meet the prevailing norms. Since the war the ideological pressure on women in the home has increased enormously and a veritable army of social workers has been trained in family case work.[31]

The family, then, is the unit to which state services choose to relate, which is reinforced and structured by local government. Housing is a case in point. Almost the only housing type that is available by direct council provision, or through council lending schemes, is the family flat or home, with just a few single-person possibilities for those who drop out of the family through age, sickness or the failure of marriage. The relationship of councils in the last few years to the homeless and to squatters has demonstrated laughable attempts to fit people into 'family' nomenclature: 'family squatters' are any household group that can rustle up a child between them; a person and child are not a person and child but a 'one-parent family'. Quite apart from cost, the state needs the family as a structure to match its own, to which to relate. One way of looking at 'family' is to see it as part of a management system. As I will suggest in due course, 'community' is best seen as part of this system too.

Financial stress and urban crisis

One consequence of the great expansion of the kind of responsibilities the state undertakes in the social formation and the increased scale at which it is called on to fulfil them has been a continuous and massive growth in state expenditure. Local authority expenditure in particular makes panic headlines: it rose from £1,528 million in 1954 to £12,778 million in 1974, approximately doubling as a proportion of the Gross Domestic Product in twenty years.[32] More important perhaps in the eyes of central government is the fact that the local authorities are spending a greater part of the total government spending of the nation – which has itself been rising as a proportion of Gross Domestic Product. Local authorities expenditure, 23 per cent of all public expenditure in 1954, was 31 per cent by 1974. The number of people employed by local authorities rose from 1·5 million to 2·5 million between 1952 and 1974 so that by this latter date local government had on its payroll no less than 11 per cent of the country's entire workforce.[33] No wonder the management of local councils has been subject to scrutiny.

Reasons for the growth in state expenditure appear to lie in two related trends: class struggle and the development of capital. First, the working class has its own interest in state spending. The welfare state, that 'post-war settlement between capital and labour', came into existence not least because of a shift in the balance of power in favour of the working class. Since its inception workers have gradually come to recognise that social welfare is part of their wage – the 'social wage' – and to press for increased provision. This pressure in particular forces the state to provide, even if only minimally, for the chronic sick and old, no longer part of the needed work force.

Second, as technology advances capital requires a more highly specialised and trained workforce: more spending is needed on education, for a start. The reproduction of the labour force is an extended job, each generation costs more to prepare for work and the state is more involved in its preparation. It is not surprising therefore to find that the fastest growing sector of state expenditure is the social services (health, housing, social welfare, social security and education) whose share of Gross National Product went up by 50 per cent in the period 1951 to 1973.[34] The long-term shift from small competitive business to national and inter-national monopolies noted in the previous chapter[35] meant that more and more people have become employees, either of business or of the state. No longer self-employed or of independent means they are at the whim of the job market and like others need state-provided social security and other services.

The processes of urbanisation have called for more spending on roads, water supplies, etc. The state has become increasingly involved in physical planning and the share of infrastructure in state spending grew in the fifties and sixties. It was a pattern reflected in other Western advanced capitalist societies. The growth and decline of modern cities is intricately connected with developments in capitalism. They are subject to inflows and outflows of capital of different kinds at different times as manufacturing, commercial, property and finance capital operate within their markets. Lambeth was a good example of this, experiencing the arrival and departure of manufacturing industry, the mushrooming and decline of property speculation, the activity in its housing programme of a local and national building industry, and so on. For capital to increase its productivity it must tend to socialise (that is to turn into a collective activity) the general conditions of capitalist accumulation. This is the role that maintains the city. The close packing of people and functions (shops, offices, banks, etc.) speeds up the movement of capital from the moment of production (at which moment alone wealth is produced) through the processes leading to consumption and thence back to investment where it can again make wealth. The city cuts down the unprofitable circulation time of capital.[36]

Many aspects of reproduction of the labour force also need to be carried on collectively.* Schools and universities demand a certain size of population. So do hospitals. Even housing is becoming a matter of collective use, because it is increasingly meaningless to separate 'house' from 'environment': water and power facilities, playspace, school, transport to work. The city is essentially a form of organisation whereby the collective activity of reproduction, that aspect of it in which the state is most involved, can be carried on. The city is as necessary to capitalist reproduction as the factory is to capitalist production. It is for this reason that the financial crisis of the state at local level has been experienced most acutely by the local authorities of the big cities, where the rate base was static or declining yet the nature of the physical environment and the condition of the population demanded above-average public spending.

Add to this the fact that state services are particularly vulnerable to inflation. Because of the nature of the work, productivity is relatively low, and difficult to raise without reducing the quality of output. Local authority trades unions have grown more militant in seeking wage increases. Besides, the national insurance scheme was designed for a period of full employment. With increasingly high levels of unemployment the delicate balance of contributions to benefits is tipped adversely. What is happening is that many of the costs of capitalist production are being socialised (paid by the state out of taxation) yet profits are private. The result is a structural gap in state finance alongside the tendency to growth.[37]

It is easy to recognise the alarm which the 'rediscovery' of poverty in the late 1960s caused to urban managers, civil servants and ministers alike. Britain had experienced the post-war boom, the

---

* The term collective is used to mean that the financial provision is no longer an individual and family responsibility. It does not mean that people necessarily undertake the activity together. Council housing is an example – it is state provision but families live in separate dwellings.

hey-day of 'you never had it so good', every family seemed to be driving a Vauxhall Victor and watching a 20-inch TV. State expenditure on social services had been rising for years. Yet an apparently ineradicable poverty continued – it seemed – to afflict millions of people, particularly those in the inner areas of large cities. It was revealed by reports of government-sponsored commissions and committees (Plowden's findings on primary school deprivation[38] were published in 1967); in the press statements of the poverty professionals (the Child Poverty Action Group exposed the Labour Party's failure to end poverty[39] in 1969 just before a general election). It showed up in homelessness ('Cathy Come Home' was screened on TV in 1966, SHELTER was formed soon after). And it began to find expression, as we shall see in the following chapter, in popular militancy and protest in cities.

Corporate management was thus a response to these two problems. On the one hand the growing need to keep down costs, to manage scarce resources as fears grew about the level of public spending. On the other the apparently undiminishing problem of deprivation, the shame of urban poverty in what was supposed to be a thriving and exemplary capitalist society.

The performance of local agencies of the state, particularly the authorities of big cities, gripped the attention of the central state in the sixties. The local councils and other authorities had to carry on their reproduction responsibilities but they had to do so at least cost – since the financing of growing state expenditure by running up debt was a dangerous long-term economic policy. Around the middle of the 1960s, what had been a nagging anxiety about levels of state spending began to turn into attempts to contain growth. Local authorities' resource problem (how to make the necessary rate increases politically palatable) was increasingly shared by central government which was supporting local councils to a growing extent through grants and subsidies. In 1954 rates represented 41 per cent of local authorities' revenue. By 1964 although rising massively in money terms they had fallen to 38 per cent and by 1974 to 30 per cent of a rapidly escalating expenditure.[40] The growing difference was made up by the centre.

Curbed financially, local authorities nonetheless had to be spurred forward to deal more effectively with urban social and economic problems. The advantage to central state planners of local authorities' financial dependency was, of course, greater control over local council budgets which in turn gave them more of a say in the way they carried out their job.

If no more money was forthcoming, policies against poverty could hardly be radically developed. What could be changed, however, was the urban management system itself. The attraction of the corporate management reforms was that they might render local councils more directly responsive to the centre, more intrinsically geared to national economic and political priorities, and provide them with the skilled financial planning and resource management that could make centrally imposed cuts and incentives effective. Further – a long shot perhaps – it was hoped to make urban policymaking sufficiently informed, intelligent and analytical to find a solution (what solution was unclear) to the scandal of urban poverty. The promise of corporate management however, in both respects far outreached its achievements.

3. Management under pressure

By 1974 Lambeth council, with four or five years of corporate management to its credit, should by all accounts have been deftly despatching the poverty dragon with one hand while reining back the charger of public spending with the other. But Lambeth, like other authorities, was finding that the new management inside the council was no match for trends whose cause lay mainly outside. What happened, in fact, during the period 1968 to 1974 was that the council's expenditure rose from £7·2 million to £17·4 million.[1] Even allowing for inflation this represents a growth of 50 per cent in six years. The sum lifted annually from the borough's ratepayers rose from £9·1 million to £21·4 million (an increase of one-third in real terms). Worse, the borough's indebtedness had trebled, going from about £39 million to a staggering £114 million in this period – a debt of £382 for every man, woman and child in the borough. Servicing this debt alone cost the council £9·6 million in 1973–74. Well over half of the total of the council's annual spending was now buying nothing new for Lambeth's population but was instead paying back the moneylenders for the loans with which they had financed past work. It is to be doubted whether corporate management even succeeded in increasing the productivity of the council's own labour force, since the number of employees also rose by one-third in these six years, ending at 5,400.[2]

And what happened to the local working class and its poverty? Unemployment had trebled.[3] The list of people waiting for a council flat had grown from 11,500 in 1969 to 15,000 in 1974. One in every four households in the borough lived in a shared dwelling. Just over half the dwellings were thought to be structurally in good condition; one in five of the borough's housing units had a life limited to 15 years. The condition of Lambeth's poorer wards in fact prompted its selection in 1971 as one of three areas in Britain to be given special study by planning consultants as part of the Department of the Environment's Inner Area Studies.

Nothing fails like success

The aim of these Inner Area Studies was to analyse the precise nature of 'multiple deprivation' in the inner city, especially as it found expression in poor housing and environment, and to think out ways in which a corporate management system could use its new-found integration to implement comprehensive, 'total approach' policies to cure it. The interest of the study for our purposes lies in its analysis of the problem. It pointed to such matters as the deteriorating job market and the price of land being root causes of deprivation.[4] Nor was the downhill progress due altogether to the *failure* of official policies – it was in some measure due to their success.

The key factor in deprivation among Lambeth's working class was low family income, resulting from high unemployment and the scarcity of well-paid jobs of a kind local people were qualified to take. It derived mainly from the operations of the market but was in part also a by-product of planned policies. The high level of unemployment in the borough is explained by a combination of processes. Lambeth is not a city but part of a city. Its economy is part of a metropolitan and national economy. It is in the nature of capitalism that development is uneven, that some areas grow at the cost of decline in others. In Britain for many decades there was a steady attraction of capital and labour to London and the South-East. It resulted in stagnation in the old industrial areas like the North-East and North-West and to housing shortage, traffic congestion and atmospheric pollution in London. After the second world war, in a planned attempt to counter this magnetic effect of London (and to a lesser extent of other cities) and to push capital and skilled labour back into the depressed regions, or to hold it there, controls were placed on industrial development in the metropolis and incentives offered elsewhere. Firms wanting to come to the London region were discouraged. Firms already here and wanting to expand were urged to move to the surrounding new towns where they would find space at less exorbitant prices and better housing for their workers.

The latter years of this policy coincided with a boom in land and property prices. As the limits to office development in the Cities of London and Westminster were reached, speculators and property developers started to look for plots south of the river. One cuckoo-in-the-nest that illustrates the trend is the lavishly appointed tower block developed and also occupied by the Finance Corporation for Industry. When this powerful institution moved out of the City of London it leased and cleared for itself a site in Waterloo where had been many poor lodging houses for single elderly people. Now the dossers and meths drinkers sit in its shade all day and many sleep out at night. There was difficulty finding a taker for the manager's luxury penthouse on top of the adjacent block. Paradoxically, the reason given by prospective clients was that the displaced dossers made the area distasteful to prospective clients.

By such processes the value of Lambeth's real estate rose so high that the remaining manufacturing firms could scarcely afford to stay. The less buoyant went broke, others continued the migration out of London. Mergers and take-overs in manufacturing industry increased the propensity of firms to rationalise their plant and often to re-locate in areas where land was cheaper and labour relatively unorganised. Central government, which had it in its power to give or withhold office development permits, was also implicated in the way things turned out. The amount of office floor space in Lambeth went up by 15 per cent between 1966 and 1973. In this same period industrial floor space declined by 22 per cent and commercial floorspace by 2·5 per cent. As a result the borough was deprived of almost a quarter of its manufacturing jobs and getting on for one-third of its commercial employment. Even the number of labouring jobs, relative to the number of unskilled workers looking for such jobs, also dropped significantly.[5] Besides, the local council too had been forced to make the problem worse by buying up for its urgent housing need land that might otherwise have continued to serve small manufacturing industries. Lambeth council's own planning studies note that if the housing redevelopment programme were to continue unamended it would affect approximately 300 firms occupying approximately one million square feet of industrial floorspace and employing three thousand people.[6]

As a result of this combination of market forces and state planning the population of Lambeth fell. It had been at its height in the early thirties, when there were more than 400,000 people living in the borough area. Since then it had continuously fallen, till by 1971 a quarter of this original population had been lost. It is important to recognise that this experience was by no means peculiar to London and Lambeth. The policy to restrict the growth of conurbations, keep 'green belts' around them and push investment into the new areas resulted in all seven of the major conurbations losing population in absolute numbers.[7]

It was not a typical cross-section of the population who moved away. The out-going people included a higher than average proportion of skilled workers in well-paid jobs who followed their firms elsewhere. To the extent that others had come into London or grown to maturity to take their place, they were the less skilled. Between 1966 and 1971 the middle ranks in Lambeth's population had fallen by a sizeable number: there were 7,000 fewer skilled manual workers, 3,500 fewer non-manual workers and 5,000 less service and semi-skilled workers. In the same period the borough gained 5,000 workers in the lowest economic category, the 'unskilled and other' workers and, at the opposite end of the scale a small number (between one and two thousand) of employers, managers, self-employed and professional people.[8]

Of the economically active a growing proportion were unemployed. As manufacturing jobs became fewer those who were able to get work tended to have to settle for low-paid jobs such as caretaking, clerical work, cleaning, van driving. In Lambeth there are many districts in the centre and north where income rates are much lower than the average for the Greater London area.[9] Those who are poorest tend to be the old, families with relatively large numbers of children and single-parent families. More married women than elsewhere go out to work (62 per cent of married women under 60 in 1971 were employed outside the home). They were working 'the double shift' not for pin-money but because they were unable to manage on the husband's wage alone.

Not only was the demographic trend towards a low-earning population, it also led to a more dependent population. The number of people of working age declined relative to the number of those they had to support. Where these workers had been 65 per cent of the total in 1961 they were only 62 per cent in 1971. The proportion of the mature working age group, those between 30 and 65, fell fastest of all. So what was left behind was a population that included old-age pensioners, more children and more young people of an age when, if they are able to take an apprenticeship or study, they are most likely to do so.

The racial composition of Lambeth's inhabitants also affected their chances. In 1966, 17 per cent of the population were born outside the United Kingdom. By 1971 this had risen to 21 per cent. The two largest ethnic groups were the Irish and the New Commonwealth immigrants, born mainly in the Caribbean – and black. These West Indians cluster in the central Brixton area and in two of these wards they make up more than one-fifth of the total population. West Indian workers had been allowed into Britain at a certain period to satisfy capital's need for cheap unskilled labour. Now in Lambeth immigrants were suffering the brunt of unemployment. In particular twice the proportion of *young* West Indians compared with other youth were out of a job.[10]

It is easier to see now in the contemporary history of Lambeth what was in the preceding chapter no more than theoretical: that capital is the prime mover in the city. It is developments in capital that are the basic forces at work; the state as a whole, in its many separate institutions, responds to and serves capital. In Lambeth the local authority carries on much 'reproductive' work for capital. It has the difficult job of coping with the contradictions thrown up by capitalist development, maintaining and reproducing the labour force, a labour force to whose upkeep *local* capital may not be making a direct contribution and in which it may even momentarily have no interest. In doing so it is subject to financial curbs and standards of performance imposed by central state agencies and has to operate within national state policies. Besides, of course, it has to confront and handle local working class militancy and pressure. Thus the political leadership of Lambeth Borough Council will from time to time protest to Whitehall and to Transport House about the low level of the housing cost yardstick or about restrictions on council programmes. Its Director of Housing may meet under the auspices of the London Boroughs Association with other Chief Officers of Inner London Boroughs to thrash out the housing problems they share that set them against the Outer London Boroughs. This division of labour in the national state apparatus in no way belies the unitary nature of the state as a whole, and its general purpose of maintaining the conditions of capitalist accumulation – a purpose which sets limits to the expectations the Lambeth working class can reasonably have of its local council.

Working class experience

In the early 1970s then the local state in Lambeth was in the position of having to service a remarkably costly population in a situation of tighter and tighter money. This was one horn of its dilemma. The other was that it faced the militancy of a working class whose interests in the borough's life were in direct conflict with those of capital but who addressed their anger mainly at the council. The scandal of their condition was rocking the boat for the local state and local people were continually threatening to evade the proper relation to authority.

People were responding to their situation in several different ways. First was the straightforward 'economic' response that can be measured in take-up of services or demand for services. More people needed social welfare, more children needed supervised playspace, nurseries, children's homes; more people went onto the housing waiting list or had to be taken into costly temporary accommodation. The second kind of response was individual direct action, an unthought-out attack on the nearest target, under pressure of an intolerable situation. Thus children damaged property in streets or on estates. The impoverished young mother took to shoplifting – an attack that was also self-defence. The incidence of crime among young people in Brixton was dramatically exposed in the press. The young blacks, whose 'delinquency' was so much deplored and feared were those school leavers who were carrying the brunt of unemployment in Brixton. At the end of the academic year 1975 it was estimated that about a thousand of the children leaving school in July would be going back into overcrowded homes and onto the streets because there was no possibility of work for them. Whatever the causes and whoever the 'criminals', the normal police force in Lambeth was reinforced in 1975 by a detachment of the Metropolitan Special Patrol Group whose hardy ways escalated the aggravation and gave rise to a Lambeth Group Against Police Repression.

The third form of working class response to an oppressive situation was organised collective action, mainly around housing and planning issues. 'Community action' of this kind grew rapidly after 1970. It is impossible to measure the growth in any formal way, but it was attested by the experience of many councillors and activists. 'Oh yes, there's been an increase in community action without a doubt. I think it is the attitude of people that's changing. They want to have a say.' 'There's been a massive increase. It's been inspired by political activists.' 'It is social change, people are demanding their rights.'

Many groups formed to defend themselves from the side effects of council redevelopment policies.[11] Activity around council tenancy increased. Groups organised against homelessness. Squatting in council and private property began around 1970 and grew on a scale that continually made national news. Many people began to find some collective strength in working together, for example in a claimants' union, organising their own playspace, or making a refuge for maltreated women. Though there was much more organised militancy than anyone had experienced outside the workplace before, there were many problems still left untouched. There was no concerted action around schools, for instance, which in Lambeth were under severe pressure from large numbers of children with language difficulties and the problem of obtaining staff to work in them for the salaries and conditions that prevailed. Nor was the inadequate health service provision in the borough challenged. The action focused mainly on housing and environment. Nonetheless this 'community' militancy had particular meaning as an expression of working class anger in a situation where industrial militancy was slight. Workplace actions were increasing in the country as a whole – to the point where the miners' strike was able to bring down the government in 1974. But in Lambeth the effect of exchanging office blocks for factories had been to leave small and scattered production units where organised action was scarce.[12]

We ought to look for a moment at the life lived by people in Lambeth. Because if the council was caught up in a contradictory situation, no less were ordinary people. The contradictions they experienced go some way to explain their animosity and the confused ways they found of expressing it. People wanted jobs; they would travel long distances to find one and would accept something far below their real level of skill just to be in employment. Yet once in work they suffered hard conditions and low pay. For many people the best they could dream of, more than they could hope for, was a council flat. Yet those who were 'lucky' enough to be in council flats found the standard of accommodation and maintenance on many estates appalling. Many tenants in formerly private houses bought out by the council found that the council was as dilatory over repairs and improvements as their old landlord had been. Besides, once in council tenure they were subject to officious control, to rules and regulations that often left them less freedom than they had had before. People needed the advice of a social worker as to how to get the best out of a complicated welfare system; yet they felt obscurely that the access a social worker had to their home put them under some kind of supervision. Many people were afraid of growing violence in the borough; they wanted the protection afforded by the police. Yet all too often it was their own sons who were done for 'sus' and their own daughters who were in court for petty theft. Finally, they needed each other's support and mutual care and yet the family was often oppressive, especially for women and children, and the housing estates for all their density are not necessarily friendly places.

Many people therefore, especially women on whom housing and family income problems bear hardest, were feeling trapped. Far from seeing the local council as a provider some were coming to identify it as the enemy. The political expression of this frustration took the form of a direct attack on the council's authority. Though the Director of Housing and the Director of Development were singled out as bogeymen, the dislike was not only for the bureaucracy but for elected members too. 'Housing chairman arrogant at meeting' reported a local news-sheet. 'The councillor's indifference to people's problems and arrogance was apparent throughout the meeting. He seemed to think that even if he was elected by the people of this ward they should solve their own problems and not bother him. He didn't seem to realise that *he* is one of our problems.'[13]

Where was confidence in the vote, the representative system, the 'party of the working class'? Instead of queuing in an orderly way for councillors' surgery sessions, instead of wording moderate petitions to be lodged in the fullness of time on the council agenda, local groups were shouting, pasting up disrespectful posters and insulting Labour councillors. A head-on conflict between the working class and the bureaucracy, mainly over housing, was outstripping the power of the Labour Party to mediate or to control. The development of a movement around homelessness and squatting dramatises the forces at work. Let's look first at the nature of that action and then move on to examine the condition of the local Labour Parties and the electoral system. Their poor shape was both symptom and cause of the council's lack of authority.

Squatting: a crisis in capitalist relations

The combination empty houses/homeless people/squatting is the housing manager's nightmare. The council's distress over the Lambeth situation was the greater because council redevelopment and rehabilitation policies initiated by the Tories and continued in the 1970s by the Labour administration had directly contributed to it. They did not *cause* it – the causes were of far greater depth and sweep. But each council measure to solve the problem seemed to have a side effect that made it worse. The bulldozers that rolled across Lambeth at the behest of the planners had (for practical reasons) destroyed many good dwellings as well as bad. They had run ahead of the capacity to rebuild, and so left many acres of rubble that housed little but rats.[14] As private landlords were bought out by the council to allow the bulldozer passage, many tenants were harrassed and winkled out of their rooms so that the landlord could get a better price for a house with vacant possession. In the improvement areas many other house owners left their dwellings unlet in the hope of getting more profit by selling them after 'gentrification' of the area. Rehabilitation itself meant putting more pressure, even if only temporarily, on the borough's housing stock as people were decanted while repairs were done. As the Labour Party increased its purchases of private houses in 1973 and 1974, not for redevelopment but for management, it acquired properties it hadn't got the resources to rehabilitate or to administer. The council was caught between market forces and government curbs and each step it took seemed to increase housing voids, increase homelessness and invite squatting.

Squatting began in Lambeth in 1971 in a moderately constitutional manner but as it progressed such procedures were abandoned. Homelessness had made national headlines in 1970 and squatting as a form of political protest had already begun in two or three areas when a handful of squatters installed themselves in empty council property in the borough.[15]

At the 1971 council elections the Labour Party had won many seats that had been expected to remain in Tory hands, particularly in Norwood constituency. The result was an unexpected proportion of left-wingers in the Labour group, young men and women who had never been councillors before and had not seriously been intended for office. For a few months they managed to have some influence on council policy and one of their victories was to obtain the vice-chairmanship of the Housing Committee (1971–73). The new vice-chairman arranged a meeting between himself, the leader (1971–73), the local squatters and two national squatter leaders. Between them they made an agreement: the squatters would form a housing association, with proper rules, and the council would provide them with a supply of short-life houses that it could not use itself. They might however, squat only people on the council's waiting list or eligible to go on it immediately. The squatters formed the Lambeth Self Help Housing Association – but became better known as the Family Squatters.

At this time the council were buying around 1,000 houses a year for eventual redevelopment. Some of these short-life properties they boarded up (20 per cent); the majority (65 per cent) they took on as council lets; but some went to the squatters. An officers' report of this period concludes 'it is considered that Lambeth's policy for dealing with short-life property is effective, receiving favourable comment from the Department of the Environment and participants'.[16]

The Housing Directorate had good reason to be satisfied with the arrangement. The Family Squatters administered their properties efficiently. They were allocated as and when they became available by the homeless themselves at regular Wednesday evening meetings. Contributions of £3 a week from each family enabled the association to cover maintenance and repair costs and everyone helped in practical work. This building work was done at no cost to the council. In other ways too the Family Squatters were conscious of doing the job of the local state. 'For a start we are saving them money, by housing families they would have had to house and by bringing a lot of children out of expensive council children's homes'. In the main the people coming into the Family Squatters in 1971 and 1972 were young couples with children, or unsupported mothers. 'Secondly, we are actually giving them money. This is because every empty house they give us they now collect rates on. At this moment we are keeping off the council's back over a hundred families who have every right in the world to be very angry at the council and that must be worth something too.'[17]

After a reshuffle in the leadership of the Labour group in 1973 the official attitude to squatting changed.[18] The ousted Leader became Housing Chairman (1973–74). He was aggressive towards squatters and aligned with the strongly anti-squatter feelings of the Housing Director (1972–74) and other housing officers. The relationship between council and squatters fell apart abruptly. The official cause for blame was that the squatters 'had never signed their agreement with us' and had 'failed to keep accounts'. It was a familiar situation. The Family Squatters' organisation was informal but effective. It had formed itself into a network of base groups on a street by street basis. It was democratic, run so far as possible by its squatter members. The council found it difficult to do business with a group that was not organised in a similar style to itself.

Now the Family Squatters had no new supply of houses and (as homeless people kept coming to them) they were forced to advise on independent squatting. The kind of people coming for help had also changed. Even elderly couples, West Indian people whose children had grown up and gone, were desperate enough to be thinking of squatting. 'If you are 56 and your kids have reached 30 you won't get a flat out of Lambeth council. You have missed the boat.'*

Meanwhile other unrecognised groups who had squatted houses began in their turn unsuccessfully to seek agreements

---

* While I was in the Family Squatters' office one such couple came to discuss the possibility of entering a house. The Family Squatters' worker was telling them how to put a knife in the window and slide the catch, how you unscrew the bolts on the door from the inside. They were tense and anxious, weighing as they listened the import of what they were about to do. Nothing in their past experience had prepared them for such a step.

for more with the council. Among them were Melting Pot (for young black people), the Railton Road Women's Centre, the Gay Centre (a mutual support group for homosexuals), and several neighbourhood councils.[19] In particular, Vassall Neighbourhood Council (one of the council's own 'community' creations) came into the squatting movement with some publicity. An unsupported mother of two teenage children, ex-homeless herself and recently rehoused from a half-way house, undertook a housing survey with others from the neighbourhood council. It revealed that on the evenings of the third and fourth of December 1973, in Vassall ward alone, 336 houses were standing empty, 106 were in the process of being demolished, 424 had been demolished within the past year and only 40 were being rehabilitated – though still empty. In all 906 houses had been lost from the housing stock and the number of new houses being built in the ward was: nil. The survey showed that the loss of dwelling unit-years in one ward in three years almost equalled the total dwelling unit gain achieved by the council in the whole borough.

Getting no response from the council to their request for accommodation these activists started to squat families. 'We called in the Self-Help Housing Group. We prefer not to call it squatting because a lot of people get the impression you are a hippy or junky or something. The majority of short-term tenants are working people, family people. It's not that we select them. They are the ones who come to us. We ask no questions.' It began with a couple of teenagers, married, with a baby and living in a van. They were brought to a neighbourhood council meeting and a decision was made to squat them in council property. By mid-1974 the Self-Help Housing Group were squatting 16 dwellings and housing 30 adults and 40 children. The woman organiser and others found it hard and trying work. 'It's not easy – often you have to do it at night, one and two o'clock in the morning, because of neighbours. It is a seven-day, 24-hour a day job. When this woman moved into Burton Road there was no piping, gas, electricity, windows or bath. It was like a shack. And we really worked on it. It is one of the best in the road now. The council don't recognise how much we do.'

The 1971 census had shown that there were 5,250 dwellings empty in the borough. Articles in the London press revealed that many of these voids belonged to a property empire, the Gerson Berger companies, belonging in the main to a single wealthy family. The council, urged by the Labour Party left wing, undertook to buy out Gerson Berger flat by flat. The news of Lambeth's empty homes in this way travelled all over London and even more squatters were attracted to the area to squat in these flats.

A new type of squatter was now involved. 'To squat private empty houses requires a different outlook. In a council squat you know where you are. To squat private houses you need to be younger and tougher.' Up to June 1973 the growth of unrecognised squatting was almost entirely in private property. This squatting of private property was sometimes a direct challenge to the council to buy the house without vacant possession, accepting the squatters as council tenants – the squatters were giving the council a lead on municipalisation. When it became known that by the council's own estimate 2,500 of the borough's empty dwellings belonged to the council itself, its piousness over Gerson Berger looked shabby. Unrecognised squatting in *council* flats and houses then grew fast.

By the summer of 1973 the realtionship between the town hall and the homeless was worse than it had ever been. 'Every six weeks the number of squatters was doubling,' said the Vice-Chairman of Housing. 'There was near hysteria in the Labour Group.' Squatting is not only a practical solution to individual housing need, it is a statement about property and ownership. As such it is a political movement. A handful of councillors on the left-wing of the Labour group welcomed it and worked actively with the squatters. In doing so they were abandoning their loyalty to the Labour Whip.[20] Apart from these renegades there were some officers and councillors of both parties who were so appalled by homelessness that they withheld judgment on the squatters' infringement of the property principle. But the dominant view was an abhorrence of squatting. Even those who tolerated other forms of activism were clear about where they drew the line.

'These squatting groups – it makes me very angry. It's outrageous, anarchical.'

'Squatters with colour TV sets – they aren't homeless, they're the *cause* of the trouble.'

'These people don't come from Lambeth, they just arrive here from Birmingham and Glasgow and expect us to rehouse them.'

'They aren't families, they're hippies. I went to see a squatted place once. We visited it as councillors. We kicked open the door. It smelt in there. There were six boys and four girls all sleeping, all doped up no doubt.'

'All squatters have nervous ticks.'

'They aren't homeless. There's nobody homeless today.'

Who were the homeless and the squatters really, and why were they so feared and hated by these men and women working for the local state? Homelessness is of course not a statistical category but rather a continually changing statement about people's hopes or despairs. There are several manifestations of homelessness. The real one is impossible to measure, being the number of people in overcrowded or dilapidated homes, or forced to cohabit with people they cannot any longer reasonably live with. A small proportion of these, those who have presented themselves as homeless to Social Services, often via the police station, are to be found in bed-and-breakfast hotels (around 90 families in Lambeth by the council's estimate in 1974) and in temporary accommodation (between two and three hundred).[21] The homeless also turn up as squatters: people who did not present themselves to the authorities but preferred, either independently or with help from squatting groups, to take over housing that was standing empty. This population is again impossible to measure, but it was thought that there were between two and three thousand by this time in Lambeth in both private and council accommodation. Finally, the only really quantifiable homeless are the family that turns up, in the flesh, with suitcase, on the town hall steps on any one day and so brings the theoretical problem to life for the Housing Committee. There were many officers and members in Lambeth in 1973 who

were alarmed by the growing number of homeless families that
were coming to light in this way.

Contrary to the councillors' assertions, very few of the
families presenting themselves as homeless came from outside the
borough. The council's own survey showed that in fact only 15 out
of 795 applications in 1972 were from people 'new to the area'.[22]
Likewise, a high proportion of squatters were people with children.
Some squatters were not second-generation manual workers but
sons and daughters of the lower middle class, some with higher
education, some unmarried and childless – so much was true.
These were, on the whole however, unemployed or in lowpaid jobs
and the privately rented accommodation they needed was
impossible to find in the borough – or indeed anywhere else in
London. The squatters felt that class divisions were invoked by the
authorities to divide and discredit them. As a Housing Committee
councillor who worked with the squatters pointed out, Lambeth
council's housing policy had concentrated (consciously or
otherwise) upon the skilled and better-off working class. These were
no longer the main housing problem in the borough. The council
now was being asked to house on the one hand the poor working
class of the area that had been in private rented accommodation,
rooms and furnished flats; and on the other a new younger
generation who had as yet acquired no settled accommodation.
Both categories were people with whom the Labour Party did not
identify, whom indeed they saw less as a constituency than as a
threat.

It was probably true that an unknown but probably quite
small proportion of Lambeth's squatters (as opposed to those
giving themselves up to the authorities as 'homeless') came from
outside the borough. The resentment in the council against such
'outsiders' is yet another illustration of the political nature of the
local authority boundary. That some squatters were not native was
in no way unique to *them*. The borough's population as a whole
was, speaking demographically, highly mobile.[23] The council's
sources of funds came 70 per cent from outside the borough. As
we've seen, the dominant class operated on the area mainly from

outside its borders. The campaign against squatters was a nation-wide campaign in which the *Sunday People* and other papers played a part that verged on the libellous. It is not to be wondered at, then, that the homeless too failed at times to notice where the borough boundary fell. This was a class, not a 'community', struggle. Nonetheless, Lambeth's urban managers (and that included police, gas, electricity, social security and other authorities that had dealings with the squatters), called upon to reimpose proper capitalist relations in the borough, took it badly that the homeless would not stand still and be counted.

In the summer of 1973 the conflict in Lambeth intensified. There were two mass squatting demonstrations. At the last Housing Committee meeting of the outgoing council in March 1974 there were 200 squatters inside and 200 more outside the council chamber. There were six police, all the corridors were jammed.

The parting shot that month of the departing leadership was an aggressive statement to the press which, while it expressed concern about empty council houses, produced evidence to minimise the council's responsibility and squarely blamed squatters for delays in the rehabilitation programme.[24] 'The recent increase in the number of illegal squatters in council property has added to the delay in bringing empty houses and flats into use,' the press statement read. 'Repair work is held up.' It also cast what squatters took to be a slur on them as a group. 'The council has received many complaints about the activities of groups of single people who are not only illegally occupying dwellings but whose noisy behaviour causes distress to neighbouring residents.' Officers were asked to report in detail on the squatting situation. The semi-official Family Squatters were asked to stand by and co-operate while the council embarked on a programme of eviction of single squatters – to whom, unlike families with children, it had no technical housing obligation.

The council's attack caused squatters to pull closer together. They developed a confederation known as All Lambeth Squatters, produced leaflets and newsletters and called regular meetings. They replied forcefully to the council in a counter-press release. 'We will not be scapegoats for the council's housing failure.' They pointed out that for every empty council house taken by squatters, eight others remained empty. They also protested at the council's attempt to force an artificial distinction on different categories of homeless: recognised and unrecognised, young and old, families and single people, squatters and those in bed-and-breakfast accommodation. All were in need of housing provision. 'We believe squatting is part of the solution to homelessness, not part of the problem. If the council think otherwise, where do they suggest we live?'

The council's control over the situation was now slight. The problem of empty houses and squatters was but one of many aspects of housing management burdening the hard-pressed directorate. The housing administration was near collapse. When Labour was returned for a second term in the spring election of 1974 the opportunity was taken to bring a fresh team into the Housing Committee. The new chairman and vice-chairwoman had been the leading personalities on the council's earlier Working Party on Homelessness. The chairman, as a social worker himself, was believed to have some understanding of the problems and a strong will to solve the crisis. A few weeks before the election the embattled and ineffective Housing Director (1972–74) left his post. He was replaced shortly afterwards by a new chief officer – a person that the new chairman had had a hand in appointing. Together they were the new hope for sorting out the administrative crisis in housing.

Council policy on squatting now took a new tack. First, the chairman announced to his committee a new approach. It was devised and approved very rapidly, with little discussion. 'Just the chairman and vice-chairman and the officers did it,' said a backbencher. It nonetheless won the support of the Labour Party. The new policy[25] involved a promise to make one more effort to bring as many as possible of the empty council dwellings back into use by means of an upward adjustment of the 'financial' yardstick by which the directorate's spending on unfit property was controlled. Now more expenditure would be allowed on 'soleing and heeling' short-life dwellings for temporary use. The new policy on the other hand, involved an intensified programme of eviction of single squatters, without any proposal to increase available accommodation for single people in the borough. It introduced a new measure of offering *licences* to squatting *families* – that is to say, to both recognised and unrecognised squatters who had children. The housing management intended phasing out the category of official, or recognised, squatting altogether. They would give no new dwellings over to any groups and they would not replace those they took away for demolition or 'rehab'. 'All council property to be managed by the council' was the new cry.

The licensing idea was described in the committee report[26] as a means of reducing criticism of the council, bringing down expenditure on bed-and-breakfast, and above all of introducing more flexibility into the council's housing management policy. 'The licence would stipulate that the accommodation provided should be wind and water tight, but would not neccessarily be to a high standard or have all facilities, e.g. baths.' The key to the new idea was the 'single offer'. The council had been afraid to house families in short-life property before because it automatically made them council tenants and thus gave them the right of refusal to several offers of alternative accommodation when the time came to move. It thus enabled them to 'jump the housing queue', giving them the full rights of tenants. Now, the new licence, unlike a tenancy 'would also make clear that the dwellings offered may be for a short period only and that other accommodation would be offered, *but without choice*, if the household has to move.' Though the household would eventually qualify for a normal full tenancy through the waiting list they might have to go through any number of short-lets first.

Officers added in their report that they saw an additional attraction in this idea of a second class tenure: it gave them a new mechanism for dealing with tenants from council flats who persisted in rent arrears or disruptive behaviour.[27] Such tenants could now be down-ranked to licensees and placed in inferior accommodation. Some time previously they had been obliged to stop evicting 'problem families' because, of course, they were obliged immediately to rehouse them. The new licence would replace a sanction they had badly missed. The chairman also recognised this advantage and welcomed it – though he worried that to use it this way might make short-life housing 'look punitive and get it a bad name'.

Squatters called a meeting in September 1974 to discuss their response to the 'licensing' proposal. At first there was some confusion among them. Some thought they should accept the council's offer. 'They are too stupid to understand' said a former Housing Chairman in interview. 'Licensing is a *restrictive* practice. It is a licence to control. The community don't know what they are accepting. Now we will have power to investigate and only people we approve will be coming in.' The Family Squatters were too experienced by now in council housing management policy to be misled. There was soon general agreement among squatting groups that the new policy should be rejected. A leaflet was put out entitled 'Licensed to Live' which explained that licensing would be a second-class form of tenure, giving no choice of accommodation on removal, no limit to the number of times a licensee might have to move before permanent rehousing could be achieved. The leaflet also pointed out that the council planned to use the licence as a punitive measure. The squatters argued that the council itself was hamstrung by government regulation and by financial interests profiteering out of housing and that, in the circumstances, those best fitted to manage empty housing were the squatters themselves.

At the end of 1974 the council policy was still hardening. Squatters were facing eviction of their non-family members from council property. The council continued cold-shouldering squatting groups and hoping to see their organisation wither. In December 1974 six hundred squatters assembled at the town hall and made six demands: (1) no eviction of tenants or squatters and rehousing for squatters when they agree to move; (2) decent housing for all – an end to the waiting list con trick;* (3) full facts

---

* Anyone qualifying was readily accepted on the Housing List and thereby encouraged to expect a council dwelling. Squatters were not alone in feeling that the expectation was false. For many on the list there was no likelihood of obtaining a council flat in their lifetime, because the demands of redevelopment and homelessness ensured that no more than a mere handful of the 15,000 were rehoused in a year from the list. The figure was seventy-one in the year 1973–74.

about the method of housing allocation; (4) council take-over of all empty private property; (5) an end to the destruction of its own property by the council; and (6) public expression of the council's opposition to amendments to the Criminal Trespass Law. This last demand is explained by the fact that the Director of Housing and many in the Labour group were known actively to be supporting the move to toughen up the legal powers of councils and other property owners to expel squatters. Lambeth council was the only local authority to give evidence to the Law Commission while it was drawing up its report on criminal trespass. A campaign against such amendment of the law was later started by All London Squatters, including squatters from Brixton, and soon became nation-wide.

The difficulties of regularising short-life lets and the directorate's alarm at the possibility of yet more squatting led during 1974 to an increase in the council's practice of sending its workmen to smash up empty houses and render them uninhabitable. This official vandalism characterises a situation where fear of people had altogether replaced commitment to the job of housing them. It was a curious expression of the contradictions in which the council found itself. All its moves against the squatters were to little avail however. Two years and a number of policy measures later there were estimated to be three thousand squatters including perhaps one thousand five hundred children in about six hundred squats. Lambeth was probably the most squatted borough in London.

The condition of 'local democracy'

One reason for the embarrassment of the state in these circumstances was that a mechanism on which management of class struggle may theoretically rely, the electoral system, lacked the power to convince local people that its procedures were worth using. This arose mainly from the weakness of the links between such people as the borough's homeless, jobless and claimants and the local Labour parties. The Labour Party is the traditional governor of Lambeth. Even during the untypical term 1968–71 when the Tories held a majority on the council many of the working class constituencies remained as they had been for decades, Labour seats. If the Labour Party does not represent working class interests on the council they are not represented at all.

Despite its 56 seats on the council Lambeth's Labour Party was by no means a mass working class party. In 1974 less than three thousand people out of a population of three *hundred* thousand were members of the party. Activism in those already small parties was very low. They tended to be controlled, especially in the poorer working class areas, by a small clique that included sitting councillors.

The electoral system is based on wards. The ward parties are grouped into constituency parties, of which the General Management Committee is the sovereign body. There are four constituencies in Lambeth borough and they vary in demographic terms and in the nature of their Labour parties. Vauxhall, Norwood and part of Lambeth Central constituency in the north of the borough were the old Metropolitan Borough of Lambeth. Labour Party people from the two southern constituencies refer to Vauxhall and Lambeth Central people as 'the northerners'. They are the safe constituencies, the old power bases of Labour's control. They cover rather similar territory: with a population of lower than average income, high unemployment, poor housing and with some private rented housing in multi-occupation together with borough and GLC council estates, both old and new.

Lambeth Central constituency Labour Party had in 1974 between six hundred and a thousand members. They did not know exactly how many. Of these about 10 per cent were estimated to be active. A turnout of no more than twenty members at a ward meeting was normal. Perhaps thirty people would help the ward party at election time. The chairman, treasurer and both vice-chairmen of the constituency party at the time of the case study were all councillors or aldermen in the town hall and all these office-holders had held their post for more than two years. One might almost say that in Lambeth Central the councillors *were* the party. Much the same goes for Vauxhall constituency, a tiny Labour

Party of between two hundred and fifty and three hundred members (1974 estimates) of whom no more than 10 per cent were active. 'It is a very quiet constituency, very quiet,' mused the secretary (in interview). 'Sons and daughters of old Labour Party people are joining us though.' Of the four office holders in this party in 1974 three were councillors or aldermen. These three had held their posts for three, four and over five years. The secretary was an old hand from the Labour Party in the North of England who kept a tight rein against leftwards or any other deviation. 'Members of my constituency are very constitutional. God help anyone straying from the narrow path.' A community worker made this comment on Vauxhall Labour Party's relation with the local population: 'The Labour Party has fuck-all relevance in the perception of the people I work with. It impinges very little on the community. The Labour Party is very weak in Vassall ward where I work. They had a hell of a lot of trouble finding three candidates for the election. One of them was dragooned.'

Streatham constituency party is somewhat different from the northern parties. In the first place it is an area with a good deal of owner-occupation and the better kind of council estate and private rented accommodation. It returned only four Labour councillors as against eleven Tories at the 1974 election. As in most marginal or Tory areas, the party had attracted a slightly younger, more professional or business-style intake. But the membership was still no more than four hundred and fifty – of whom once more about 10 per cent were, by the secretary's estimate, active. The Streatham Labour Party saw itself as middle-of-the-road, but the comment from a Norwood councillor (see below) gives an alternative perspective: 'They are rightists in Streatham. They are all friends. The grossest incompetence in the ranks is tolerated in order to avoid splitting them.' The leadership of the Lambeth council (Leader, Whip and the few others commonly referred to by councillors in interview as having special influence in the Labour Group on council) were members of the Streatham party. They were not necessarily elected for Streatham wards, however, because Streatham 'exports' candidates to the moribund northern constituencies. Nonetheless a new style seemed to be coming to the Streatham party and the wind was blowing against the council clique. None of the constituency office holders were councillors and a rule had been introduced that no officer might serve more than two consecutive years.

Norwood constituency Labour Party, in political terms, stands out clearly from the rest for its left-wing tradition. We saw the way some Norwood councillors worked with the squatters in Lambeth. The party also played a part in the council's 'community approach' – just what will be discussed in Chapter 5. The area is a mixture of private-rented accommodation, owner occupation and council estates. The Labour Party in Norwood had 1,042 members in 1973: they do actually keep a record there. It had won an untypical number of seats from the Tories at the 1971 election but this majority had later been whittled down. They do a lot of active recruiting and fund-raising for propaganda and for fighting elections. They have, in fact, a classical 'marginal' character. Members of the party including the leadership are typically in their twenties and thirties, mainly teachers and professionals. The party has a more purposeful and intrusive relationship with local popular organisations than other Labour parties. 'We get our councillors active quickly in new street groups and tenants associations as they emerge.' The agent felt that the party's recognition of the importance of such groups had not advanced far enough. 'I'd like to see Labour involved in decision-making in them, though not controlling them or taking them over.' In fact, Norwood, being a relatively dynamic party, could afford to 'use' local activists with a support base in tenant associations, etc., to curb the strength of councillors. Norwood have a scornful view of the northern parties that are in councillors' pockets. 'They are caucus parties, cliques after their own self-perpetuation. They contribute nothing to the Labour movement as a whole. They have very low membership and are run and controlled by a few people who don't encourage new membership because they want the power to themselves. They would be threatened by a large active membership. It happens in areas where there is a strong majority.' In the north, once you're elected to council you stay there. 'Councillors are councillors for three hundred years up there.' The animosity is returned. A northern secretary said of Norwood 'they are militant and pass extreme resolutions. They act "en bloc". People get pissed off with it.'

For those who are unfamiliar with Labour Party procedure it may be worth briefly describing the way that councillors get to be councillors. The truth has little in common with the myth of 'local democracy'. Before each election a panel of potential candidates is drawn up by the Local Government Committee – a committee representing all the constituency parties in the borough. Ward parties put forward, via their constituency party, the names and biographies of any individuals they would like considered as nominees. The way wards themselves decide on the names they will put forward for the panel is fairly haphazard. 'At local government level nomination is anyone who is interested. There are no criteria operating at all. Just before the election, when the selection of candidates is done, the criteria are tighter. We want someone who'll be conscientious. They must be able. They must be capable of going into council and not letting the officers run the place' (Norwood Labour Party agent).

Just before election time the party machinery 'is dusted down and rolled out for action' as a local sceptic put it. 'The only time it sees the light of day.' The ward meets and decides on a short-list, say six people. But wards where Labour is most likely to win get first pick of the borough's candidates. They notify all their members (that is statutory) that a selection meeting is to be held on such and such a date. At the cycle of meetings before the 1974 election the turnout in Norwood to these selection meetings was thirty people on average in each of the five wards. And that was the highest attendance of all the four constituencies. The six people (or however many have been placed on the short list) speak for ten minutes each and answer questions for ten minutes more. They are then chosen by secret ballot. 'It can be disgraceful,' said the Norwood agent. 'I've seen wards where no one was standing except three experienced councillors and one other. And this other was really apologetic, implied that he was there " just for the sake of appearances and please on no account vote for me".' There are several successive ballots until three candidates are in a clear majority. These three then become the ward candidates to stand against the Tories at the ensuing council election.

The representational picture is not convincing, then, for occupants of the poorer areas of Lambeth where unskilled and semi-skilled workers and their families predominate and where the worst of the problems are found. As an individual if you don't fancy joining the Labour Party there is no way you can influence the choice of a candidate for the council. And many do not wish to join: the Labour parties in those areas are moribund. Where activist councillors do represent them, they are often not local people at all but more highly educated professional, academic or business people imported from the constituency parties of the better-off areas.

Taken as a whole, if the constituency parties' estimates are to be believed (and they are more likely to be an exaggeration than an underestimate) around three hundred people *in all* in 1974 were actively involved in the Labour Party in the borough and probably no more than a dozen office-holders really kept this party machine ticking over. Nomination and selection procedures were arbitrary. In a safe ward in the centre or the north, where there is no doubt at all that all three Labour candidates will be returned to council, thirty people between them decide who shall be the councillors for the area. To the extent that candidates are hard to find in such areas, it may even be fair to say that a councillor can choose him or herself.

The turnout at the elections, likewise, is normally very low. In 1971 in Lambeth the poll was 36·8 per cent of the eligible population – which placed them about a third of the way up the London league table in terms of turnout.[28] The worst areas in London of course are entrenched Tory or Labour strongholds such as Kensington and Chelsea or Tower Hamlets where the poll is down in the 20 per cents. In Lambeth the poll varied from one constituency to another. The safe ones, Lambeth Central and Vauxhall, naturally had the lowest, with 33 and 35 per cent respectively. Even the activist Norwood only pulled out 42·5 per cent of the electors.[29]

It is hardly surprising then that the expression of the extremes of dissatisfaction being felt by many working class people in Lambeth was not being limited to the occasional surgery held in the ward by Labour Party councillors, nor lobbying members in the town hall, nor to petitions and deputations to committees and to council. The Labour Party and the ballot box were considered by many people to be irrelevant.

The situation described here is in many ways a bad situation from the point of view of the working class. More pointedly, for this particular story, however, it is unhealthy for the local state and for dominant class interests. A healthy Labour Party, holding the enthusiasm of the local electorate, pulling the people out to vote, fielding councillors who have a close relationship with local people and local groups, may be a tiger for the local bureaucracy to ride. Nonetheless it helps to smooth the path of state policies and legitimate the way quite other forces seek to run local affairs. The Labour Party was clearly not playing this part in Lambeth. As we've seen, the new management system in the town hall was if anything making matters worse in respect of 'democracy', since the leader and the busy committee chairmen were wrapped up in management priorities and the ordinary backbencher could exert little pull on this co-ordinated and closed council machinery on behalf of his or her constituents.

Where the Labour Party fails, other mechanisms must be found. A study of city Labour parties published in 1971[30] revealed a very similar situation to that existing in Lambeth, together with a similar rise in popular activism and militancy in the city. The author concluded 'to a large extent every electoral system is a sort of confidence trick and the maintenance of legitimacy through such tricks is a basic concern to all governments. When these tricks fail, as they are increasingly likely to, governments can be expected to resort to other measures. . . . In particular attempts may be made to defuse the situation by offering some form of participation or by the appointment of community development officers.'

I believe it is in this light that we have to see Lambeth

council's endeavours in community development, the apparent opening up of committee business to press and public, the sponsoring of advice centres, involving tenants in council house policy and management, employing community workers and setting up neighbourhood councils. We shall discuss this policy in more detail in Chapter 5. On a larger scale these phenomena were a reason for the state's prolific experiments between 1969 and 1974 which are discussed under the theme 'the community approach' in Chapter 4.

There is another factor that compounded the problems of the urban managers in Lambeth, however, and which certainly also pointed to a 'community' solution. Electoral democracy is only one of the bulwarks of capitalism. The family, as defined by bourgeois ideology and practice, is another. And the family was also failing in Lambeth. It was not taking its full and expected share in either reproducing the labour force or in reproducing class relations. It was failing in many cases quite inadvertently and often to the cost of the people themselves.

In the first place it was failing demographically, so to speak. The decline in the borough's population was accompanied by a trend towards smaller households. The number of single person households rose from 20 to 27 per cent of all households in the previous ten years. Here was no family at all. Then again, 58 per cent of all Lambeth's households in 1971 were of only one or two persons and many of these were unsupported mothers with one child. The state was thus obliged to deal with many people who were not being serviced or supported within a conventional marriage. Those households with five, six or seven members in the family, often struggling on a low income (the council's 'problem families') remained a constant proportion of the whole. The standard nuclear family, that considered most viable by the authorities, declined quite markedly from 36 per cent to 30 per cent of all households in the decade. The Lambeth 'family' was no longer in a position to fulfil its reproductive obligations without considerable support.

Secondly, it was failing in some cases to behave in proper family ways. Bourgeois family ideology was at risk. Driven by housing famine, as we've seen, many people were squatting. In squats (usually whole terraced houses big enough to hold seven or eight individuals) people were tending to live more communally, in groups containing both married and unmarried people, with and without children. Besides, in streets where many of the houses were squatted, the several households, sharing a situation verging on the illegal and harassed in common by authorities ranging from the electricity board to the police, began to live in a more co-operative and mutually supportive style than families are normally accustomed to do. These innovations affected only a tiny proportion of people in the borough but they disturbed officialdom. Certainly many squatters themselves believed that it was their abandonment of proper family practices as much as their occupation of council property that caused the council to come down so heavily on them.

Some women were abandoning the family altogether, and they may well have represented the tip of an iceberg in a situation where poverty and cramped housing conditions put severe pressure on domestic relationships. A particular form of homelessness is that experienced by women who are forced to run away from violent husbands who, as men, normally combine a capability for physical intimidation with legal tenure of flat or house. More and more, such battered women, seeing squatting as a possible escape, were approaching the squatting organisations for help during 1971 and 1972. They were in need not only of homes but of emotional support and advice on such matters as regaining children from the husband – things which squatting alone couldn't provide. Women from the Brixton area started a refuge in a squatted house which in a very short time had as many as 40 children and their mothers in residence and the turnover of women through this temporary refuge continued to increase. In some cases children went too – in others they went into council 'care'. The number of children in the council's care for this and other reasons rose by 50 per cent between 1968 and 1974.[31]

Finally, the family was failing the state in its inability or unwillingness to control children and teenagers. The increasing incidence of truancy, vandalism, petty theft and mugging weighed heavily on the nerves of parents, fearful of the outcome for their children. But it nonetheless also represented a way in which the state was picking up a problem of control that in other circumstances would have remained that of the family.

Such a critical situation out in the streets and homes of Lambeth made *corporate management* in the town hall, pre-occupied with balancing the books, investigating the productivity of its typists and making sophisticated long-range projections of its inability to house the population, seem an inadequate reform of urban management. For all its promise of tougher control of resources, more penetrating analysis of social and economic problems and co-ordinated policies to solve them, it was beyond the powers of the new corporate management system of the council to arrest the deterioration of local people's circumstances. Worse, it was if anything exacerbating their disrespect for the authority of the council. The corporate reforms were not, however, the only aspect of the new management in local authorities. The other side of the coin was called 'the community approach'.

4. The community approach

Management by extension

Local government managers are not alone, as is often supposed, in having a population and environment 'out there' to administer. Business firms too, though they do not have the state's statutory responsibility to govern the people nonetheless have clearcut interests in influencing the way people behave. The monopoly enterprise in present-day capitalism has one quality that above all else distinguishes it from the smaller competitive firm. It has grown to include among its goals some measure of control over the consumer. 'The initiative in deciding what is to be produced comes not from the sovereign consumer who, through the market, issues the instructions that bend the productive mechanism to his ultimate will. Rather it comes from the great producing organisation which reaches forward to control the markets that it is presumed to serve and, beyond, to bend the customer to its needs.'[1] This manipulation of the consumer by the giant corporations arises not as some mean-minded conspiracy but because that is the way such firms have to behave, operating as they do in an uncertain environment. State organisations too are growing in size and in the complexity of their role in capitalism. Their environment is also increasingly uncertain. Lambeth is not very different from other urban areas in experiencing shifts in economic circumstances, changes in working class demands. So the state too seeks to 'bend the customer to its needs', the needs of government.

Whereas the firm tries to reduce market uncertainty by controlling demand, by intelligent advertising and judicious product-design, the state uses participatory democracy and 'the community approach'. The applications may be different but the causes are similar and so are the means: *both are phases of corporate decision-making*. The connection between the community approach and corporate management will become clearer if we go back briefly to planning and its use of systems and cybernetics.[2] The science of systems both guides and explains the practice of giant corporations. By getting inside the thought-processes of capitalism for a moment we may better see what is happening within its institutions, because systems theory increasingly is used to guide state behaviour too.[3]

One of the key ideas in cybernetics and the control of systems is that control is closely related to information flows. Indeed it is so closely related as to be almost the same thing. The amount of information flowing within and between systems largely determines the ability of a system to control itself and the influence it can exert on its environment, on other related systems. In a human system like a local council this can be anything from a legal decree or government circular to the chat that flows down the phone connection between one officer's desk and another's. Human systems, human beings or organisations, are defined as 'open systems' because they are in continual interaction with their environment.[4] Of outstanding importance to an open system is the information that flows across the boundaries between itself and its environment . . . wherever these are presumed to lie. 'Viable systems maintain equilibrial behaviour only by multiple contact with whatever lies outside themselves.' That is a fundamental law of systems theory.[5]

A simple example will show how crucial to a system's control of its environment is information. Many man-made machines and all viable systems are equipped with a homeostat which uses information obtained from its own operation and from the environment to guide the correction of its own behaviour and bring it back to normal. The thermostat in a central heating system is an example. The thermostat uses information about temperature (the room is too hot) and responds by switching off the energy supply until new information (the room is now too cold), fed back into the system, reactivates it.

Cybernetic theory suggests that the more complex the systems being controlled the richer the channels and flows of information that are needed if the control system is to be up to the job.[6] Judged by this criterion, strong hierarchies of the kind produced by corporate management reforms in local government are far too inward-looking. Their connections with their environments, though theoretically they are many (70 councillors and aldermen and many officers working in daily contact with the public) are nonetheless in practice not very efficient as sources of 'feedback', nor are there appropriate mechanisms to gather, organise and channel this information back to the brain-box of the Directors' Board for decision-making. Besides, corporate management in its local government form pushes control up to the top. All the information tends to go in one dimension only, travelling up and down the hierarchy but not across it. It reaches the top in a crudely simplified form. This design may be a solution to the problem of integration and internal control of money and manpower, viewed in a narrow and short-term way, but it is a bad design for a system in what the theorists call a turbulent environment – and that of the local state is increasingly turbulent.[7] It needs more fertile cross-connections at the bottom-end between its internal parts – between the social worker, the rent officer, the public health officer.[8] It is also a bad design for innovation, it doesn't induce new ideas.[9] It hinders rather than encourages 'learning' and adaptation in the system.[10]

A systems theorist such as those who advise big corporations would propose that the system comprised by the state, as a whole or taken unit by unit, can only behave appropriately for its own survival and exercise control over the related system of the local population if the information flowing between the two is rich, varied and continuous. This raises the question, of course, as to where the boundaries of the system are deemed to lie. In systems theory the boundary between one system and another is unclear. Systems by definition include one another and overlap. 'A system is not something given in nature, it is defined by intelligence.'[11] The distinction between systems and environment is relatively easy to make in a small business firm. The system is the company itself, its shareholders, executives and workers – the organisation which produces and sells the goods. The environment is the supplier, the other companies in competition, and the market.

Taking this systems view, a local council adopting the traditional low-profile, the administrative role, can be defined as a self-contained system – with the 'clients' as part of the environment. But as local authorities are geared up to govern more assertively they may implicitly be defining the authority and the governed population, for some purposes, as falling within one and the same system. The 'people' are in there alongside, though obviously distinct from, the state's workers. An interesting endorsement of this idea has come from the application of systems theory to local development planning: 'the two systems overlap to some extent . . . for example, community action may be thought of as arising within the urban system and seeking to change the kind, pace and direction of change currently pursued by the planning system. If community groups become institutionalised they may then be best understood as forming part of the planning system itself; and the substantive results of their actions . . . would then be regarded as changes in the urban systems themselves.'[12] Local government's reformers have seen this inclusion of community into state as a *goal*. 'The most difficult problems do not lie in the integration of the decision-making in the local authority but in the integration of the community and the corporation,' wrote one of the consultant firms.

The state, like a corporation, looks for ways of 'influencing the environment so that its own present or future behaviour is more efficient.'[13] One of the ways is to incorporate bits of the environment into the system, by increasing the information flows and other practical links between the two. It is by integrating the local population into predictable 'families' and 'community groups' and by setting up 'joint committees' between itself and them that the state can develop the level of information flow that amounts to 'governance'. In this it is little different from the corporation and its customers. It is in this light that we should look at government proposals for 'participation' and community development. The proposals of the Seebohm Committee with regard to the reorganisation of the social services provides an example. The committee's report[14] called for maximum involvement of 'individuals and groups in the community in the planning, organisation and provision of the social services'. Foster-parents could be used to recruit other foster-parents, old people could help run their own clubs, mothers be involved in caring for their own children in hospital. Now – in making use of state services one does not necessarily become part of the system – in sharing in their administration one may well do so.

The point is this. The potential control of the state increases the more closely the working population is knit to the state system. We should think for the moment not of overtly repressive control but simply of management of the working class, its 'families' and 'groups' in the business of reproduction of the labour force and of capitalist relations. But this incorporation of the population is a two-edged sword for the state (and for the working class). Because the closer working class groups come to inclusion within the state system, the more dangerous is any disruptive behaviour to the equilibrium of the state. The state has reduced risk in one way but increased it in another. Imagine how a linking up of the workers within the state and the serviced population, also now 'in' the state, would threaten control. Changes in the way the state system adapts to its environment in this way represent new phases in class struggle.

The fact is that local government has been evolving and adapting its relations with its environment. Alongside the internal shift to corporate management, just a year or two behind in most cases, has come a restructuring of relations with the community. Councils have made a show of opening up the local state decision-making process more to public view, encouraged the local population to organise into groups and arranged more, carefully structured, interaction between such groups and the town hall –

supposedly inviting them to share in urban management functions. Above all they have been trying to embellish the role of the local councillor, the contact man with the 'community'. They have been appointing community development workers to link up town hall and 'community' and also to forge links across service departments at the point of contact with the local population.

Central government has had a similar part in this development to the role it has played in the development of corporate management in local government – analysing the problem, foreseeing new ways of doing things, encouraging and prompting local councils. Indeed in this it has gone further and actually carried out joint experiments with selected councils. In this chapter I describe central government's part, choosing a few initiatives for closer study. Accounts of central government measures and the supporting work of academic and professional institutions are relatively explicit and the management meaning of the 'community approach' comes through quite clearly. It is possible to see how community development theory evolved in the same period as corporate management theory and in how many ways they complement and endorse each other. Subsequently I will look at the same approach in operation in Lambeth.

One further reminder is necessary. The difficulty about thinking and writing about the state in capitalism is that the effort to escape from the prevailing ideology sometimes leads to seeing the state in crudely mechanistic terms. When we identify the advantages to the state and capitalism in a certain course of action, when we look for possible motives, it seems to imply that some mastermind is at work – foreseeing, planning and pre-empting. The truth is not like this, as daily practice makes more than clear. Movement and change in social formations stem from both sides in the class struggle; one move leads to a counter-move. We saw something of the class situation in Lambeth, the pressures on the local council from the disorderly and spontaneous reactions of the working class population to their experience of oppression. It was in response to such pressures as these that the 'community package' was evolved. Central government's measures occurred as a set of discrete policies; they occurred as a series of steps and changed their emphasis over time in response to changes in the balance of class forces. One led to another. Or rather the failure of one led to another. The state was trying to seize the initiative in a period when the relationships of governors to governed was being challenged. Local people wanted participation; local councils saw advantage in 'participation' if it was on their terms. Local people wanted collective strength; local state saw advantage in 'community', but one made in its own image. If there lay management advantages in these things it was because the management problem had grown. In this account the main focus is the local authority and consequently the efforts of the working class and those who tried to pursue working class interests from within the state, though they are important, have not been heavily emphasised. It is the tactics and strategies of the state that we most need to understand. It is a corrective to the idea that the state's offers of participation and community development are gains *in themselves* for the working class. Rather, they are what the working class can make them. They lead class struggle one step onward and bring new dangers *and* new opportunities. Among the local state's employees and local councillors who were involved in implementing these measures there was a wide range of hopes and intentions. Some frankly, others less frankly, wanted a more sure and controllable situation in which to govern. But many aimed to win what they could for 'the community' from within the state system.

A seat at the table

In 1968 'the May events' shook France and toppled de Gaulle. In the same year the Ministry of Housing and Local Government in London set up a committee under the chairmanship of an MP, A.M.Skeffington. The two happenings, though they did not have the same news-appeal, were not unrelated. Students and workers in France took for a moment by direct action, with a violence that threatened the regime, the control they wanted over the institutions in which they worked or studied. Similar demands were being made on British institutions though they were more modestly expressed. So it was a timely period for the government to explore ways in which local councils could afford the population more of a say in state decision-making. Skeffington was asked 'to consider and report on the best methods, including publicity, of securing the participation of the public at the formative stage in the making of development plans for their area.'

The proposals put forward in *People and Planning*[15] were addressed mainly to local councils as planning authorities and they were quickly taken up by councils faced with a statutory obligation under the Town and Country Planning Act 1968 to consult the public over structure plans – a responsibility they were unsure how to fulfil. Within a few years they were competing with each other for the laurels of 'best participator'. Susan Cooper describes the campaign launched by Worcestershire, one of the first authorities to produce its structure plan under the new legislation: 'It had taken three months and covered 14 centres. An exhibition of the proposed structure plans was shown in all those centres, manned permanently by three of the council's staff. Altogether 7,958 people went through the exhibition, with 2,660 returning their comments: these are now being processed and will go before the council, which will then decide whether or not to amend the plans. In conjunction with the exhibition, 800 people attended public meetings in the 14 centres.'[16] Worcestershire, like Teesside, Merseyside and other large planning authorities used marketing and public relations consultants from the world of private business to set up their participation campaigns, conduct surveys and so on. The Department of the Environment itself paid for Merseyside's market research and sent its own civil servant to evaluate the exercise. A more cost-conscious approach was to use the public and community groups to undertake opinion surveys, as did the Greater London Council in its partnership with Golborne Neighbourhood Council over the Swinbrook action area.[17]

The management principles embodied in the Skeffington Report were, first, to make *implementation* of plans easier by preparing the public in advance. Participation would produce 'an understanding and co-operative public. If objections can be anticipated or eliminated the formal stage of public enquiry will be smoother, less contentious and speedier'. Secondly, there was a legitimating purpose. Participation could bring people into a friendlier acceptance of local authority. A plan could be 'a bridge instead of a barrier'. Skeffington insisted that participation in planning should reinforce local electoral democracy – the councillor should be more involved.[18]

Skeffington's recommendations were taken to have wider relevance than physical planning alone. How could these advantages be obtained, not just in planning, but across the board of local state activities? In particular, how could they be obtained without the local councils losing more than they gained from a management point of view? Merely to open the town hall door an inch or two was not enough. It would be a disruptive and uncomfortable experience for officers and councillors unless there were some form of organisation into which the chaos of popular action could be structured. An interface of some kind was needed to mediate between people in great numbers and the state in its unity, a device to order and transmit the information flowing between population and local state. Skeffington devised the idea of a community forum for what he called 'corporate discussions' of local interests. The form in which this idea was eventually taken up, was the *neighbourhood council*, or *community council*.

The need for some kind of small-scale 'democratic' counter-balance to larger, rationalised local authorities was recognised at the early stages of local government reorganisation. The Redcliffe-Maud Commission devised and recommended, as we saw in Chapter 1, a system of local government that involved, for most of England and Wales, a single tier system of large unitary authorities. Along with this centralising, co-ordinative measure the commission put forward the idea of local or community councils. They were not to be involved in the statutory servicing tasks of local government. In that sense they were not management bodies. But in another sense they *were* to be management bodies, because they were intended to manage the relationship between governors and governed. They were to be a 'democratic' complement to the more centralised authorities.

> Local councils should be elected to represent and communicate the wishes of cities, towns and villages in all matters of special concern to the inhabitants . . . the only duty of the local council would be to represent local opinion, but it would have the right to be consulted on matters of special interest to its inhabitants and it would have the power to do for the local community a number of things best done locally.[19]

As the government proceeded via White Paper to legislation for local government reorganisation, however, it became clear that, while provision was going to be made for 'successor parishes' in the rural areas, they were reluctant to give neighbourhood or community councils in urban areas any statutory form. So in 1970 a group of well-connected campaigners set up an Association for Neighbourhood Councils (ANC) to press the government to establish an urban counterpart to parish councils as part of the reform arrangements. 'Community feeling is not the prerogative of villages alone,' they insisted.[20] In spite of the efforts of the ANC, the 1972 Act did not include provision for statutory urban neighbourhood councils in England – though community councils *were* provided for under the separate legislation for Wales and Scotland where the Wheatley Commission had urged, more strongly than Redcliffe-Maud, 'a broadly-based unit with an official standing, to which the local community as a whole can give allegiance and through which it can speak and act.'[21] Meantime a number of areas were experimenting with unofficial neighbourhood councils. The first fully elected council was in the Golborne Ward of North Kensington. Liverpool Southern Neighbourhood Council and, as we shall see, those of Lambeth Borough Council provided other examples.

It is important to recognise that those who were striving to get neighbourhood councils constitutionally adopted were by no means *against* the centralising, co-ordinative reforms of local government as a whole. Indeed Michael Young (chairman of ANC) specifically wanted to avoid his pressure group leading to any reopening of the debate about reform as a whole, 'that might imperil the whole grand scheme which the country has already been awaiting much too long'.[22] Tough, corporate, rational urban management was not being *rejected*. What was being asked for was an equally management-minded 'democratic' initiative, a complement to the new bigger local authorities very much along the lines that systems theory would have predicted.

We should look for a moment at the nature of the new body being proposed by the ANC. The Association were looking for a new mechanism 'so that ordinary working people can participate in their own "local" Local Government and so assert the needs of themselves and the communities to which they belong.' But underlying this aim was no sense at all of the real division of interests in society, between classes and between fractions of capital, between the local state and some of the groups it was called on to govern. The new bodies were to paper over the cracks: 'Towards One Nation: A Nation of Good Neighbours'.[23] Neighbourhood councils should seek to represent public opinion 'in the decision-making processes of an increasingly complex society. They should be of great help to the ward councillor anxious to consult with local opinion, and to local authorities generally.' Systems language was used. The NCs could amplify 'deficient feedback' from the governed population.

There were some in central government who also saw the advantages in the idea of more structure, more 'membership' in localities. The Rt. Hon. John Silkin, Minister for Planning and Local Government in the Labour Government of 1974 took up the matter of neighbourhood councils with personal enthusiasm. He had led the opposition to the Tories' Local Government Act 1972, moving an amendment calling for statutory neighbourhood councils. Under his direction the Department of the Environment sent out a consultation paper[24] to the local authority associations, the ANC and political parties, asking for advice on the question of making neighbourhood councils available by right to any community of between three and ten thousand who might petition for one. The aims that the Department had for neighbourhood councils are pretty significant and worth quoting.

> (a) to organise or stimulate self-help within the local community to improve the quality of life for the residents as a whole (for instance by clearing dumped material from derelict sites);
> (b) to help those in the community in need of special facilities (for instance by providing play-groups);
> (c) to represent to operational organisations (central and local government, firms with factories in the area, etc.) the needs and wishes of the local community;
> (d) in doing all these things, to foster a sense of community responsibility in the residents, particularly for children and adolescents whose potential for idealism it may help to harness.

It is all there: saving on public expenditure; building up a corporate community point of view to match the inter-corporate decision process of the state bodies, including gas and electricity corporations and local capital; and the creation of a sense of membership – all with strong ideological overtones.[25]

Silkin had seen the management advantages to councils of such outposts, reconnoitring in the 'community'. 'From the council's point of view, the neighbourhood council should be seen as their watch dog, telling them about local conditions and wishes, problems, etc., in a more detailed and intimate way than (they) could ever find out otherwise, alerting them to the need for action, and perhaps most important, warning them vociferously when things start to go wrong; that is something all of us in any local government need. . . .'[26] The Department of the Environment added to this perception an understanding that 'democracy' needed a facelift. They specifically recognised the anti-'democratic' nature of corporate management. 'Current trends in management thinking in local government are liable to absorb the individual councillor into the general work of the council to a greater extent.' They also foresaw a management-sharing relationship. 'The general pattern might be for the council to provide funds, skilled staff and premises, whilst the neighbourhood council provides local knowledge, local organisation and voluntary help.'

We could look at any of a number of different types of mechanism devised in this way by central and local government to make 'participation' happen. One more example will stand for others: *tenant involvement in council estate management*. This is something still unresolved, but another straw that shows the way the wind blows. In August 1974 the Minister for Housing and Construction appointed a working party to report among other things on housing co-operatives. Housing co-ops were seen as a possible way of enabling tenants of local authority and housing association estates to 'participate collectively in decisions which affect them'.[27] A Department circular followed the Working Party's report urging local authorities to sound out their tenants.[28] There seemed to be two thoughts in the corporate mind of the Department of the Environment. One was cost-saving. 'Particularly at a time when it is important to use managerial and financial resources more efficiently, and not increase rate or subsidy costs unduly, the introduction of co-operative schemes could be a means of bringing additional personal resources into housing.' Local authorities should only go ahead if they could be sure that at the very least no additional expenditure would be incurred. The other thought was to lessen the management burdens bearing on local housing authorities. 'By developing a stronger sense of community and by enabling tenants to exercise real control over their living conditions, co-operatives should be able to reduce some of the problems too often encountered by tenants, such as social isolation and poor housing management.' This kind of management gain, however, would depend on 'realisation by tenants of the responsibilities involved'. The Department seemed to have feared that local authorities might go too far and grab too readily at a chance to unload themselves of some knotty problems (known more intimately in the housing management profession as problem *families*) and warned 'it is essential that (the scheme) should not be seen simply as a means of relinquishing responsibility for problem estates or for functions which are proving troublesome.' The idea was full co-operation between local authority and tenants' group, including sharing the right to nominate people to tenancies. The circular was taken as an opportunity to press the idea of participation in general. 'Where conditions are not suitable for co-operatives, tenants should nevertheless be involved through consultation and participation in the running of their homes.'

Just to emphasise once more that 'participation' is not only a new opportunity for pressing working class interests, nor only a means for the state of reaping ideological gains, but also a strictly nuts-and-bolts management affair, I will quote from an article in a local governmental journal, a pep-talk to backward housing managers on the advantages of tenant management.

> Authorities themselves have much to gain. Nowhere can the benefits be more obvious than in the housing field – in establishing good relations with tenants. This is the key to the smooth running of council estates, which is essentially a team operation. If tenants choose to be difficult and obstructive, they can make the housing manager's job a nightmare. They can also add thousands to the costs of administration and maintenance.[29]

The faces of community work

Making provision for 'participation' is one thing. Getting the working class population to take its seat at the table is another. When the local state looked around them they found plenty of the better-off groups who were ready and willing to do business with them: civic societies, preservation societies, residents' groups. They participated without prompting. But the poorer working class, the sufferers of 'urban deprivation', did not immediately make use of the new opportunities. It was they who were the main clients of social services and housing services in the cities. It was they who most often posed a threat to the orderly relations of production by direct action, individual or collective. Yet the very nature of councils and committees, the style of the Labour Party, the class affiliations of senior officers, all set local government apart from the poorer working class and made them an un-knowable factor in government.[30] 'Participation' therefore naturally led to community development, the official initiative to ensure working class engagement in local affairs by fostering community 'membership' in poor areas. Community workers, community development officers, liaison officers, community relations officers, many such appointments were made in urban authorities between 1968 and 1974.

Although the great increase in community work activity dates from the 1960s, its practice goes back at least to the foundation in the nineteenth century of University Settlements such as Cambridge House and Toynbee Hall in deprived areas of London, bringing privileged intellectuals into working class neighbourhoods to live alongside and raise the cultural level of local provision. No doubt it was also a practice of the Christian church long before that.

In the post-war period it is the state that has taken up and developed community work. The earliest introduction of community development programmes was in the colonial context in India and Africa, where its purpose was to 'help' people living in traditional societies to adapt to the modern technology and culture introduced from Europe.[31] It pays to reflect on that early practice, far from the metropolitan inner city: it was the progressive face of colonial rule, much as here it is the progressive face of urban management. A second source of these ideas was the Ingleby Committee Report of 1960[32] and the Children and Young Persons Act 1963 and the subsequent work of the Children's Service of the Home Office, with its Family Advice Centres in deprived areas.[33] Third, there was the Seebohm Report – already mentioned many times – which led to the extension of community work in the Welfare State through the Local Authority Social Services Act 1970. Finally came a decade of development of the community work profession sponsored by the charitable trust of a private capitalist foundation, the Calouste Gulbenkian Foundation between 1963 and 1973. The National Institute of Social Work Training was a partner in this, and in the latter years community workers themselves have grown in numbers and strength of purpose and have continued their own development in the new Association of Community Workers.[34]

Community work makes a fruitful but a very painful and difficult study when approached from within our frame of reference. It is useful because it demonstrates quite dramatically the way that the state and capital can sometimes benefit from and exploit or disarm progressive ideas and progressive people. It is painful because the literature and the practice are peopled with fine humanitarian and radical motives and it is hard to propose that this work may sometimes have an effect other than that which was intended. The headache arises from the effort of always forcing oneself out of the dominant ideology and into a recognition of the objective relationship of community workers, community development funds and projects, to the state and to capital. And in recognising that though community work does bring with it new situations and new opportunities for working class gain, it also sometimes leads working class groups into incorporation and impotence.

Community work is so richly documented and the interpretations of community work so very diverse that I have picked out just three tendencies for illustration. I shall try to show how each of the three – the *social pathology* approach, the *social planning approach* and the *conflict method* – represent a development of urban management technique in response to a developing urban management challenge.

First, an account that illustrates the classic formula for community work that has come to be known as the *social pathology* approach. It awakens alarm and disgust in exponents of other tendencies of community work but is nonetheless far from being discredited or discontinued. Aryeh Leissner and Jenifer Joslin describe the progress of a community work exercise that grew out of a neighbourhood-based Family Advice Centre (FAC).[35] This particular phase or brand of community work is specially interesting because of what it illustrates of the state's relationship to the family and most of all to women. The FACs worked at the point where the family function was failing. They are the classic example of the local state's intervention in and partnership with the family for purposes of reproducing the labour force (healthy upbringing) and of the relations of production (avoiding delinquency, crime and disaffection). The criteria for designation of FAC areas was 'a high percentage of low-income, unskilled or semi-skilled workers' families, a great number of large families and many families in the area receiving state income supplements'. The high-need criteria also included 'a high incidence of truancy, learning difficulties, retardation, other physical and emotional handicaps and delinquency among the children of the area, a high percentage of one-parent families, inadequate school facilities and a high rate of teacher turnover, as well as a significant proportion of immigrant families, substandard, overcrowded and badly maintained housing and a lack of adequate and easily accessible shopping facilities.' Multiple deprivation, as it was to be called a few years later. Home, as many people in Lambeth would have recognised it.

The approach of the particular FAC with which Leissner and Joslin were concerned was to 'help the community to revitalise a defunct tenants association, to provide recreational services for children, teenagers and adults, to initiate self-help activities and neighbourly assistance for the elderly and to improve relations between the community and the handful of immigrant families living on the estate.' Among other family-supplementing activities of the FAC was the organising of a mothers' group which 'plans and takes its annual holidays together and organises a number of social events throughout the year' for parents and children.

The technique seems to have involved getting working class families to recognise that they were failing, out of their own income and capabilities, to provide facilities for their children to acceptable standards. Such families were encouraged to 'recognise' the difference between the two standards, to express a need, such as for recreational programmes for children, arts and crafts centres, pre-school playgroups, facilities for the elderly ... and then to organise, with the prudent help of the FAC, to provide for themselves. 'For the delinquent as well as for the withdrawn youngsters and for their families the FAC's potentialities for an integrated availability of recreational programming, advice, guidance and assistance and community work can provide a very valuable service.' But the community must not long depend on the FAC. The community itself, the new enlarged responsible 'family', must stand on its own feet. 'The goal is community autonomy.' The community was to fend for itself; but at the same time the community group, this newly organised unofficial social welfare agency, could become part of the local state. By the end of Leissner and Joslin's story, the mothers' group had 'moved into the area team offices', and 'sees itself as part of the area team without any noticeable change in its community identity'.

An explicit aim of the project described here was 'to identify and acknowledge areas of conflict in order to resolve conflict and prevent it from spreading'. The authors of the report describe the community worker's role as 'social diagnostician'. It is as though conflict were a cancer, to be caught early. This approach to community work takes its cue from social work. If the case worker says to the family 'you are the problem', the community worker says to the 'community', 'you are the solution'. You will help us (the authorities) to raise the standard of performance of these families to a satisfactory level, the bourgeois standard to which it must operate if it is to fulfil its reproductive purpose in a capitalist society. You will also, incidentally, save us the cost of institutional care in mental hospitals, children's homes and so on. You, the community, will become an enlarged family, likewise with our help becoming functional and independent. As you do so you will find you become almost a part of the authority.

The second community work approach I want to illustrate is the *social planning* approach. It was the central message of the second Gulbenkian Report[36] which was produced by a study group chaired by Dame Eileen Younghusband. This interpretation of community work is closely related to the introduction of corporate management and planning into the operation of the local authority as a whole. The Gulbenkian study group and the Maud Committee on management in local government were doing their work in the same period, the mid-sixties and published their reports within a year of each other. Typically, the community worker in question is an employee of the local council, not necessarily in social services, often in some central unit, perhaps attached to the Chief Executive. Within this frame of reference there are differences of opinion among community work authorities as to whether the emphasis should be on the development of professional community workers doing a specific community development job, or on the development in professionals and administrators in other services such as housing and planning of a 'community orientation' that will affect the work of the council as a whole. There is a striking similarity between such discussions and those in corporate management and planning as to whether corporate planners ought to be distinct professionals with their own unit or whether they should be dispersed to develop a 'corporate orientation' in other services such as Treasurers, Education or Housing. Younghusband concluded that 'there is a strong case for a certain number of well-qualified community workers whose appointments would be built into the local, regional or national power structure.'[37]

A further parallel between corporate planning and this 'social planning' style of community work is the emphasis on both comprehensiveness and integration, 'seeing things as a whole'. 'The need in community planning is to think in terms of whole persons and of the satisfaction of their needs as persons in social interaction with each other, rather than focus attention on a series of separate needs and problems. This suggests that community work as an approach to people's social needs *has its necessary counterpart in an integrated approach to planning* and administration at national, regional and local levels.'[38]

To illustrate the role of a community worker involved in this kind of activity I'll quote from an interview with Liverpool Corporation's newly appointed Community Development Officer. He explains that his job involves assessing

> what is happening in community work in the city, particularly in relation to the roles played by voluntary organisations. In the authority itself I have to coordinate the role for community work

between the different departments. This means examining how the different departments function and, if necessary, suggesting how existing resources could be redeployed. I am also a reference point for community organisations who want to find out what the local authority is doing, and for the authority which wants to keep tabs on the different projects going on in the city . . . I spend half my time working with the different departments of the corporation helping them to think through ways of informing the public and meeting them, and redefining jobs to make sure some of the officers have a *specific function relating to the community*. The rest is spent with community groups, tenants associations, community councils, voluntary, church and university organisations trying to bring about the maximum cooperation between them, and with the council.[39]

This social planning approach to community work calls on social science research. It is the market for instance for the statistical 'social indicators' developed by academic social scientists to help planners to identify areas of deprivation and stress.[40] It serves the information needs of management: 'grassroots community workers are part of the close and continuous two-way contact which is needed between various groups in the community and the statutory and voluntary organisations'.[41] Liverpool's Community Development Officer, and others like him are corporate agents operating at the periphery of the system, organising corporate behaviour in the community, encouraging community-oriented behaviour in the local state and fixing up interaction between the two. It is a far cry from Leissner and Joslin's home helps.

Increasingly over the last five or six years community workers, trained in universities and colleges of the state, financed and employed by the state, are encouraged or at the very least not prohibited when they choose to get involved in community organisation leading to protest and political activism. Why? Many community workers would make a cut-off point here and say that *conflict method* community work is not doing the job of state and capital at all, but is 'running away with the salary cheque'. On the face of it this style of official community work *is* the most difficult to understand in terms of the management needs of the local state. This is what I believe has been happening.

For various reasons already explored the working class in inner urban areas have become increasingly dissatisfied over local council services that they receive at home – as well as being increasingly militant at work. The partial opening of local council doors to 'participation' and the early expenditure on community work and community development have by no means always worked out in the best interests of councils. We saw that this step was bound to be more of a high-risk, high-gain move than was corporate management for the local state. Many community workers and other state workers have learned from their exposure to 'multiple deprivation' and drawn their own conclusions. 'They have gone native' (as a councillor in Lambeth put it), given their loyalties wholly to the working class locality in which they work and held their job security lightly.

Nonetheless the state needs community workers for the many reasons we've seen. So, in spite of the risk of explosive conflict (between local authority and activist groups, between officers and members and between traditional and progressive members) the local council does not always pull in its horns, nor do community workers who are into conflict always get the sack. Instead the conflict is moderated and converted, wherever possible, into a style of governance. There are two ways in which conflict, in small amounts and certain contexts, can help maintain equilibrium in capitalist society. First, it can de-fuse a situation leading to greater and more fundamental conflicts. Thus D.V.Donnison, now Chairman of the Supplementary Benefits Commission, proposing a scheme of decentralised local service centres to help overcome the problems of specially poor areas, sees their aim not as neutralising social conflict: 'on the contrary, their aim is to promote more productive conflict and furnish procedures for successive, temporary arbitrations and agreements.' He looks for better opportunities for local people to seek their rights and make their demands heard. 'It is the politicians' task *to manage conflict* not to eliminate it.'[42] Second, a degree of conflict safely contained in the electoral representative arena can reedem the idea of democracy. It makes it seem as though a genuine class struggle were taking place through the vote. Too much apathy and quietism – and the system appears a charade losing its ability to legitimate the state in people's eyes.

A reflection of this pragmatic reality in British urban politics can be seen in the more academic field of political science. In the mid-1960s the prevailing theory of democracy was superseded by a somewhat different view of society and politics. It had been argued since the 1930s and before that the only realistic way, and indeed the only safe way, to govern in capitalist society was through elites. If the ordinary person were to be given any more involvement than that of voting it would either come to nothing due to his apathy or come to totalitarianism due to the workers' vulnerability to fascism.[43] But in the 1960s political scientists began to revive the classical idea of participatory democracy: people should and could be much more directly involved in the institutions in which they lived and worked or which governed them.[44] The picture of society that accompanied the new theory of participatory democracy portrayed a nation of many different interest groups, more or less evenly matched, competing in an institutionalised manner for resources and powers.[45] For such a system to be viable it was necessary to suppose that society was in no way fundamentally riven by class conflict. In this context, conflict method community work, then, if it could hardly be seen as bringing working class groups to sit at the table, could nonetheless be seen as bringing them armed to the arena. It would not be an arena of conflict between the dominant class and the exploited class, but rather a tournament between small groups more closely related to each other: within the working class and its near neighbours – those 'contradictory class locations' between the working class and the true bourgeoisie.[46] They shake out as tenants, mothers, ratepayers, teenage youth, house owners, swimming enthusiasts and squatters. All are asked to compete and defend their special interests against each other, while the class with the real power remains untouched and out of earshot.

All the three styles of community work described here co-exist today – and exist alongside other variants. But there has nonetheless been a progression. It can be seen in the three reports sponsored between 1963 and 1973 by the Gulbenkian Foundation.[47] The first[48] had very much the sort of whist-drive philosophy favoured by the voluntary social work agencies. 'People are enjoying themselves, for few community development schemes succeed without lots of festivity, dances and parties. People are also learning the meaning of citizenship in a changing society,' and so on and so on. The phrase 'citizenship in a changing society' is identical to the rhetoric of the community development projects that characterised the last years of British colonial rule in Ghana and other territories.[49] The second[50] as we saw opted quite strongly for the social planning approach. And the third[51] is different again. Now community work is about the 'sharing and redistribution of power in any given society or community in pursuit of the search for greater social equality and social justice ... a concern with distribution of resources, benefits, power and influence.' Gulbenkian Number Three recognises conflict at the outset.

> Local communities now protest more frequently in strength against changes made without consultation or insist, if necessary by demonstration, on local or central authorities hearing their grievances or allegations of neglect or indifference. Increasingly, such protest is directed against the effects on local communities of the socially arbitrary decisions of big business or nationalised industry, for instance in re-location or technological development. The democratic right to protest and be heard and answered by those in power has a very long history in this country; but its recent exercise has become more widespread, more emphatic and often more effective. Community groups have been making it clear that they can and will hold authority directly to account and expect a proper hearing and a reasoned response. In this climate of rapid change a greater or lesser degree of *conflict is inevitable and often healthy.*[52]

Community work thus takes on the mal-functioning bureaucracy, the atrophied electoral democratic system and attempts, by its conflict method, to force it to respond – to adapt. To adapt – to survive. Enlightened civil servants and ministers are not averse to local authorities getting the odd jolt into modernity. As we shall see they deliver some of the jolts themselves. Even progressive members and officers in local councils share this far-sighted tolerance, as we shall see of Lambeth. A responsive local authority, while it may be logically impossible in capitalist society, is yet its ideal.[53]

The spur to innovate

So community work and community development grew, both as a profession and an aspect of the welfare state, through the initiative and support of central government. Many local authorities were, not surprisingly perhaps, slow to catch on. The community approach is a tiger that conventional councils are unlikely to mount without some hesitation and a bit of prodding. In order to learn more rapidly and in a more controlled and experimental way about these departures in social policy central government set up a number of projects in local areas. These projects enabled it to intervene directly, joining in partnership with certain local authorities to develop the new community approach to local authority services.

I've chosen just four schemes out of many to illustrate central government's tutelage of local government. They are the *Educational Priority* exercise (which began in 1968, sponsored by the Department of Education and Science); the Home Office *Community Development Project* (1969); the *Comprehensive Community Programmes* (1974) again out of the Home Office stable; and the *Area Management Trials* (1974) by the Department of the Environment. They are chosen because they demonstrate the gradual merging of the central government's community development policies with its corporate management policies. Beginning apparently from different perspectives, two sets of civil servants, one in the Home Office and one in the Department of the Environment, found themselves confronted by the same reality: the need to save money; cure poverty; pre-empt working class militancy. And gradually they found they needed each other's policies if they were to create effective urban governance.

The first three schemes illustrated here use the action research method, the government's new probe, pulled from the tool kit around 1969. They were 'co-operative ventures between local and central government in research and policy development'.[54] Action research means introducing some changes into practice and accompanying this practice with research – practical research to help the action along, to help it to know where to start and what to do, plus evaluative research to show what the outcomes were. What we are seeing is the planning principle entering *national* social policy at much the same time as it was changing the style of physical development decisions (the structure planning cycle) and local state business as a whole (corporate planning).

The *Educational Priority* exercise originates in the Plowden Report on primary education, one of those that, in the late sixties, helped to 'rediscover' poverty.[55] Recording concern over areas 'where educational handicaps are reinforced by social handicaps in the home and environment', it identified what later became known as the poverty-cycle, or multiple deprivation. The language is reminiscent of William Beveridge – great reformers share this compassion and noble style. Lady Plowden evoked 'the seamless web of circumstance' and the 'ingrained dirt of generations'. The 1944 Education Act had been intended finally to equalise opportunity yet it had somehow, twenty years later, left untouched areas of profound underprivilege. Plowden recommended a policy of positive discrimination in education in favour of such deprived areas, based on the primary schools. It introduced the idea of the 'community school', which was, at this stage, quite a modest suggestion. 'We mean a school which is open beyond the ordinary school hours for the use of children, their parents and, exceptionally, for other members of the community.' The government adopted the Plowden policy of 'positive discrimination'. Department of Education and Science set out for local authorities the criteria for designating Educational Priority Areas and in 1968–70 backed a special EPA building programme for physical improvements to schools in the selected areas. An extra allowance was paid to teachers to encourage them to come to work (and stick it out) in the sad, bad schools. The Department of Health and Social Security and the Social Science Research Council found £175,000 to set up a special study of five of the EPAs.[56] The solution could not be, as those who tried soon discovered, more of the same kind of education. New curricula had to be devised that were better fitted to the interests of working class children. But besides work on the curriculum, the EPA teams tried to restructure the relationship of the education service and the local people through the medium of the primary school, the 'community school'.

> By establishing school-community interconnections, it constructs a stable basis upon which a three-cornered partnership of parent, teacher and child might harmoniously operate. The Community School ventures out into the community. The Community School welcomes in the community. Ideally, the barriers would collapse completely and the borders become indistinguishably blurred. Physically, one might foresee a time when, architecturally, the school, along with all other social agencies, might be subsumed into the community.[57]

Again we face a contradiction. We *need* more sensitive, caring education over which we have more say. Yet it is important to make the *effort* to remember that education described in this way is nonetheless a *reproductive function* performed for capital and in this way human ends become distorted. The money, the teacher training, the curricula are furnished by the state and serve state policy. If the school is 'subsumed into the community', given what we know of the state, is the community not also in some sense subsumed into *it*?

A number of other strands in the EPA story should be drawn out because they relate to my main theme. We can see the involvement of local state with the functioning of the family; and the raising of the sights from 'family group' to 'community group' as a focus of the proper attention of the state. We can see the seeking of a great impact for local state services, in this case education, whose impact on the poor areas was previously scandalously slight. The part played by education in the 'reproduction of labour power' is of course self-evident, perhaps easier to recognise even than the part played by housing and health services.

Finally, there is also the notion of making democracy seem less of a sham. Eric Midwinter, reporting on the Liverpool EPA, wrote in fact:

> there is a circular argument surrounding the promulgation of democracy. Can the individual be trusted to exercise democratic power fully or must he be content with his quintennial excursion to the polling station; if he be given sovereign power, will the efficiency and productivity of our society be undermined because of his lack of know-how and his insufficiency of responsibility? We tend to keep democracy at arm's length, or, rather, at ballot-box length. It seems we cannot afford the risk of popular as opposed to constitutional democracy; naturally, the only way to discover the truth of the argument is to give it a try, but we flinch from this.[58]

The fact that the children, once educated, free from alienation, full of civic sense and eagerly seizing every opportunity to vote and to participate, are nonetheless still waged workers (perhaps unemployed), still tenants in a capitalist system is nowhere pointed out. What bearing this status may have on their gains from 'democracy' is a question not raised by the Educational Priority debates.

Those responsible for the EPA scheme concluded that 'one cannot have community education without community development and one cannot have community development without community education'. This reinforced the government in its own experiments in community development: the Home Office *Community Development Project* (CDP).[59] It was set up in 1969 by a Labour Government. The aim was: 'to find, through experiments in social action, how to effect a lasting improvement in social situations which display many symptoms of individual, family and community mal-functioning.'[60] This phrase illustrates that CDP began work with a strong social pathology bent. The problems of deprivation were located in individual, family and community failure.

Each of the twelve Community Development Projects had a local action team run from a local office, sponsored (25 per cent) by the relevant local authority. The action teams were appointed to the staff of the local council. But central government paid the remaining 75 per cent of these costs and 100 per cent of the costs of the associated research teams, based at nearby universities and colleges. As with the EPA, the research teams were given a rather open brief which appeared to include research in the service of the local team (that is, research about the local area, local authority and national context of the neighbourhood) and research in the service of the Home Office (about the functioning of the action unit as an experiment). 'The lessons learned can then be fed back into social policy, planning and administration both at central and local level.'

The Home Office had its own central CDP team and a central research unit to begin with. CDP policy was originally based on the idea (as one of the CDP workers recalled later) that 'general poverty in Britain was well on the way to being eradicated and that its stubborn persistence in a relatively small number of geographical areas could be eliminated by a concentrated focus upon them.' Also implicit in the national project was central government's belief that local councils, alone and unaided, were failing to co-ordinate their services into effective tools of policy and failing to make them accessible and responsive to the needs of deprived areas. Tutoring by central government might improve local state performance.

CDP was designed to fit into the post-Maud phase of management-happy local government.

> In the past, official reports to analyse and meet social needs in the interlinked fields of employment, income security, housing, general environmental planning, health provision, social work, education, leisure facilities and so on were largely compartmentalised. Nowadays, however, the number of compartments is gradually

diminishing (e.g. through developments like Seebohm); and their degree of separation is also lessening (e.g. through improvements in the techniques of planning and management). The CDP seeks to identify and demonstrate, by reference to the problems of selected small local communities, some practical ways of taking this trend further, through consultation and action among the separate departments of central and local government and voluntary organisations and the people of the local communities themselves. It attempts this not by disrupting, supplanting or duplicating any of the work of the existing agencies, but by trying to help them and the communities they serve to develop insights. In particular it aims to reinforce and not to damage the spirit and efforts of elective local government.[61]

The operations of local teams were to have five main components: assessment of needs, stimulation of local residents to take responsibility, thinking up innovations involving community and authority, trials of some of these 'to plug immediate gaps in local social provision', and finally feeding back 'to wherever policy is formed' ideas for solutions beyond local grasp. Elected councillors and local officials were to be heavily involved. This formula was devised in the American Poverty Programme[62] and characteristic of many of the elements of the 'community package'. CDP illustrates a number of points that are relevant to our theme. One is the purposeful intrusion of government into local state affairs. CDPs were the tip of a lever the central state could bring to bear on local government. CDP workers have pointed out that in the early days of CDP, Home Office civil servants were frequently to be seen out in the field, cautiously roughing it with the lads, wining and dining them on Home Office expense accounts. Not only was it one of the devices by which central government geared up the local state to govern. It was a source of information for central state – which needs information about *its* environment every bit as much as the local council does about the local situation.

Second, there is the unusually clear-cut element in CDP of social control, the management of unrest. It was set up by Callaghan soon after Enoch Powell's 'Rivers of Blood' speech had awoken racialist aggression in areas, mainly in inner cities, where immigrants had settled in large numbers. It was introduced alongside restrictive immigration laws. It was acknowledged that the government was looking in CDP for new ways of convincing the poor, white and black alike, that it was doing something about the deprived circumstances in which they were condemned to compete for jobs and housing. In this way CDP has to be seen as related with and complementary to the work of the National Committee for Commonwealth Immigrants and the funding of local Community Relations Committees.[63]

Third, however, CDP is an example of the high-risk approach of the state being turned to good use by collective action of its workers. From the state's point of view, something went wrong with this experiment. We've shown that local and, even more, national government is prepared to go through the furnace of community protest, fanned up by community development, if it can believe that in the long run, out of the flames will come a tempered and flexible new electoral democratic local government. Unfortunately, protest and direct action went too far for some local authorities who hosted CDPs. But more significant, the analytical publications produced by the projects towards the end of their time-span were probably what finally disenchanted the Home Office. Many of the twelve project action teams, experiencing the realities of deprivation and armed with a research potential, analysed the situation of the populations in which they were based and soon moved on from the social pathology model to finish up with an 'assumption that social problems arise from a fundamental conflict of interests between groups or classes in society. The problems are defined mainly in terms of inequalities in the distribution of power and the focus of change is thus on the centres of organised power (both private and public). The main tactic is organisation and raising the levels of consciousness.'[64]

Findings from many areas pointed in the same direction. Groups chose to come together in inter-project working on topics like housing and employment. The development of a shared understanding was hastened by the creation in 1973 at the project's request of a CDP Information and Intelligence Unit, which also got papers published, circulated and reviewed. The Home Office began to cool in its enthusiasm for CDP and took various steps to dissociate itself from the running of the projects, leaving responsibility more to the local authorities. Reports expressing project findings were not reacted to, projects complained that they just tended to disappear in the Home Office machinery and concluded, no doubt correctly, that the Home Office was being a Frankenstein – it didn't want to know its child.

The account so far leaves out a number of other high level initiatives concerned with the urban local authority and its inability to see an end to deprivation. There was Sir Keith Joseph's *Cycle of Deprivation* exercise (1972), which drew in the Department of Health and Social Security, the Department of Education and Science, the Social Science Research Council and the National Children's Bureau. This scheme was deeply involved in 'family management' and included studies of 'preparation for parenthood'. There was the Department of the Environment's *Quality of Life Studies* (1974). The Greater London Council also did its little bit with some *Deprived Area Projects* in London boroughs (1973). It is important to recall them – even if it would be laborious to describe them all – because it emphasises the fact that 'the community approach' was not one or two isolated schemes but amounted to a movement involving several ministries, many local authorities, and consultants, universities and voluntary bodies. Even supra-national government got into the act with the European Economic Community's *Poverty Programme*[65] which did some work in Scotland. A number of Home Office and Department of the Environment projects were given the name 'the total approach' because they aimed to cure poverty by concentrating resources of many different kinds on a small area. One of these was the *Neighbourhoods Scheme* of the Home Office launched in June 1971.[66] Then in March 1972 the Department of the Environment announced its twin-pack *Urban Guidelines Studies* and *Inner Area Studies*, which used the services of consultants. One of the latter as we've seen was in Lambeth.

It is not surprising that observers got that *déja vu* feeling when they read in the papers on 19 July 1974 that 'the government have decided on a new strategy for tackling urban deprivation'. It was the Home Office once more, outbidding the Department of the Environment's IASs with their CCPs. Roy Jenkins' Comprehensive Community Programmes, brought out soon after Labour came back to power, was a policy already prepared by the Urban Deprivation Unit created by the Tories. 'The CCPs', said the press notice,[67] 'will identify and analyse the whole range of economic, social and physical or environmental problems of the area and contain proposals for action to deal with these problems within a five-year time scale.'

Seven local authorities at the outset (perhaps as many as seventy later on) would be invited to set up a team of three or four staff under the supervision of the Chief Executive, guided and paid for by the Home Office. This was felt to be fertile ground for the CCPs because the Chief Executives, having unlike the old town clerks no department of their own, would be glad of them as a little bit of extra personal power. The team would diagnose the situation in a selected small area (10,000 population). Quite explicitly this time central government had hit on the need for some mechanism *that could see corporate policy carried through to the point of practice*. The CCP teams would be doing research and policy-planning in the first instance but would stay on to become implementation teams. The 'community approach' is now circling back to the centre of decision-making and trying to instil there an outward-looking, impact-seeking consciousness.

CCPs are specially interesting because they mark a shift away from the belief that had come with the first reluctant re-discovery of poverty in 1968–69, that poverty was concentrated in a few small areas. The document put out by the Home Office for discussion with interested local councils explicitly says urban deprivation is '*not* concentrated in a limited number of small, easily identifiable areas . . . its causes and symptoms vary from one part of the country to another.' The Home Office were convinced that CDP-type bootstraps operations and spending-sprees like the

Neighbourhood Schemes would no longer do. All hope had been given up by 1974 of a short cut to dealing with urban deprivation. This time the teams would be trying to 'direct the major programmes and policies of government to those most in need'. Statutory approvals, loan sanctions and specific grants to the local authorities concerned would all be considered through this framework. The CCP would be 'an integral part of the local authorities' budgeting and decision-making cycle, corporate planning system and committee machinery'. It would have its own annual cycle and its own provision for public participation. Above all the new initiative would be an inter-corporate effort between central government and the two tiers of local government; the Area Health Authorities and other state bodies, which would be represented on a steering panel. Central government departments too would attempt a corporate approach in which, as many local authorities pointed out, they lagged far behind their pupils. This time they were to 'act jointly', co-ordinating central government's response through the medium of the Economic Planning Boards for the regions concerned.

The *Area Management Trials* should be allowed to bring this account to an end – though it is certainly not the real end of the central state's efforts to fit out its local agencies for government. In September 1974 Charles Morris, Minister of Urban Affairs in the Department of the Environment put the ball back in the Home Office's court (to use a civil service metaphor) with an announcement of a set of field trials concerning 'area management'. As *The Guardian*[68] put it, the exercise was to 'see if this is the answer to town hall helplessness in the face of the complex interlinked problems and needs which fall through the net of conventionally managed public services.'

Now several authorities had already been experimenting independently with co-ordinated devolution of town hall service functions to area offices or boards – or they were on the point of doing so. Stockport Borough Council was well ahead of the field by approving in 1970 a scheme with area co-ordinators, designed by their consultants Booz Allen and Hamilton. Sunderland's corporate management team were independently trying to 'extend corporate management to ward level'. The Department of the Environment now said, 'area management can also be seen as a natural development . . . of the new approach to local government organisation embodied in the Bains report and the Urban Guidelines Studies, extending the corporate approach on which they laid stress at the centre down to an area level.'[69] The basic features of area management would be 'firstly, co-ordination of the council's activities at area level by a fulltime manager, who is also a point of access for local groups, and secondly some kind of political representation of area management in the committee structure of the Council.' It was to be a way of knitting the ward councillor, out there on the periphery, hopefully in daily contact with the local population, back into the fabric of the management structure.

The aim should be to 'analyse problems, formulate policies and monitor their effects in a corporate way at an area level; operate services more sensitively to local needs by better evaluating their performance; provide a convenient channel of communication between the council and neighbourhood councils, residents' associations and other groups and individuals; (and) provide a framework in which elected members can relate council policies to local case-work and vice versa'. One of the objectives of Liverpool's Area Management project was 'the development of local democracy'.

With the announcement of the trials, DoE asked the local authorities to report on their experience and consider taking part in a series of monitored exercises. The department was to help with the administrative costs in the, by now, traditional proportion 3 : 1. Several councils responded, including Dudley Borough Council, The London Borough of Haringey, and the never-failing Liverpool Corporation which must have some of the most totally approached and focused-upon deprived small areas in Britain. No extra money was going to be spent on the poor areas this time. Indeed there was no particular focus on deprivation in this programme at all. What remained was the small-area focus and the democratic rhetoric. In area management the two halves of the new management, corporate management and the community approach, finally clicked together.

This, then, was the community package. It did not cost much money.[70] It was not a *substitute* policy in housing, health, education or any of the other servicing tasks of the local state. It was a series of research and development exercises, intended to get better value for the money local authorities normally spend each year. Corporate management had concentrated on the internal management structure of councils. The central state's 'community package' was to make good its shortcomings – first by reviving, renewing, reproducing the relations of authority; second by concentrating on implementing policies; third by providing the sources of information about the working class needed by management.

5. Whose initiative?

Reformers in the central state sowed the wind – but it was the officers and councillors of local government who were left to reap the whirlwind. Because for every advantage accruing to the state from the community approach there was a price exacted by the working class, and it was paid locally. In Lambeth council by 1974 there were many who wished they had never heard of participation.

Lambeth's community approach began about 1971, by which time the corporate management structure was in place and the corporate planning process already in its second cycle. That it happened then rather than sooner was probably due partly to the fact that the challenge from the local population only then began seriously to point up the weaknesses of the existing management system; and partly to the fact that the Tory leadership had preferred electoral democracy in the old style. The deputy leader of the Tory group on council (1968–71) (whom I interviewed in his contemporary role of leader of the opposition) said, 'It is fashionable this "responsiveness". But it is short-term and harmful. I would rather be divorced from the howls of the community, because I know how I have to act.' The statutory consultation procedures connected with housing and town planning were being carried out, but otherwise the traditional link between Lambeth council and its population (basically the vote and the local newspaper) was little modified by the time the Conservatives lost power at the 1971 election. Yet four years later at the time of this study, after one and a half terms of Labour rule, there was an extensive range of 'community' measures in operation of which the council was quite proud. They had a reputation for being, with Camden, Islington and a handful of others, among London's most 'progressive' boroughs. What had happened in the interval?

First steps in participation

The pressure for the community approach had come from three directions. Local organisations were beginning to expect more consultation. Groups of residents in redevelopment areas, feeling pushed about by the planners, demanded more information about what was happening to them and a more co-operative style from the Directorate of Development. The director, they complained, could scarcely be told apart from one of his own bulldozers. 'A few years ago,' said the Chief Planning Officer in 1974, 'I thought we were doing well if we produced a simple pamphlet. We were doing more than was needed if we held any kind of public meeting. Now there is a basic commitment to talk to people, both while devising and implementing plans.' The Lambeth Borough Estates Group, the umbrella organisation for tenants' associations on council estates, was asking for participation in housing management. 'We are looking for an effective voice on those council committees that are dealing with housing. As consumers we know the problems,' said the secretary. This had the effect of getting Joint Area Housing Committees set up on which tenants sat with councillors and it gave tenants a couple of seats on the Housing Management Sub-Committee. Squatters too were beginning to look for an agreement with the council for the use of short-life property in the borough.

The second factor was events in the Labour Party. Norwood constituency party, with its younger and more left-wing membership, was casting around for a grassroots revival. A councillor recalled, 'Everybody was saying that the Labour Party should increase involvement with the community, that people ought to be into self-help to prevent the destruction of the communities.' So the Norwood constituency proposed the inclusion of a scheme for *neighbourhood councils* in the Labour Party manifesto for the 1971 election. It seems that the Labour parties throughout the borough were also aware of a need for an alternative source of contact with the population to supplement their weak membership base – because the proposal passed through the Local Government Committee of the party with little debate. Participation was a current watchword with the Labour Party nationally.[1]

When Labour came back after the election, with a much larger majority than expected, the Norwood candidates in their marginal seats came too. They were therefore in a position for this community-minded manifesto to be implemented. The Norwood councillor who was most committed to community development was elected deputy leader (1971–74) in the share-out of offices following the election. He was the left's man-near-the-top. 'We were all talking about participation, devolving power to the community,' he said. He got the agreeement of the Labour group to apply to the Home Office for an Urban Aid grant for the neighbourhood councils scheme and, when he obtained it, the scheme won its place in the Corporate Plan without further debate.

The third factor prompting Lambeth's community approach was the national movement behind which central government departments were putting their shoulder. Participation in town planning and the opening up of council committees to press and public were statutory requirements by 1972. Community workers were the accepted thing in the new Seebohm-style Social Service Directorates. Indeed Lambeth's set of eight community workers were employed almost as a matter of nation-wide practice, without any separate discussion in the Labour group. Neighbourhood councils were being widely canvassed. Unlike corporate management, however, the idea of community development was *not* greeted very warmly by senior officers. The bureaucracy made clear that this was 'the members' thing'.

Apart from the fact that for entirely practical political reasons they needed to try out some such scheme as neighbourhood councils, councillors were aware too (so much is clear from the original documents on the scheme) of the national climate of opinion and the Whitehall-inspired measures which made Lambeth's own proposals part of a much wider experiment. This feeling of high-level endorsement of what they were about to do certainly carried any doubting members along. 'There is kudos in it. After all the neighbourhood council thing may go statutory in a few years and people here want the credit for having tried it. If it comes, they want to be already on the relevant committee. They don't want to oppose openly for fear of ridicule later', said the deputy leader.

We've seen the reasons, essentially management reasons, underlying the central sponsorship of community development. In Lambeth the new Labour leadership and the bureaucracy naturally set about interpreting the community approach in ways most likely to bring advantages for urban management. In physical planning the new ways severely taxed the officer. Most public meetings, it was felt, should be attended by the Director, Assistant Director or the Chief Planning Officer (CPO), because lower grade personnel could not know the facts nor have the experience to handle what were often challenging and embarrassing situations. 'The council didn't realise how it would go off like a bomb. Departments have scarcely got the staff resources to cope with the meetings,' said the CPO. But it was clear that participation could help the Directorate by mobilising opinion in favour of their policies. 'If plans are to be successfully implemented they need a wide measure of public support.' It was generally believed, both inside and outside the council, that physical plans were little changed by participation. 'Physical development is not very responsive. You can't change plans in midstream' (CPO).

The popular reaction to the opening of all council committee meetings to press and public left officers and members bemused. It did not fulfil their hopes of a packed public gallery quietly admiring the cut and thrust of committee debate. Instead, nobody much came at all, except when important local issues were at stake, when public order was threatened. 'It has caused the abandonment of two housing committee meetings and led to the fall of a chairman. When you have to get the police here to keep the meeting going, it can really drive nails into a political coffin.' But the advantages to 'democracy' were clear to nearly everyone. And the system adapted to the new situation: members and officers learned to operate the two-stage meeting. Committee agendas were split into two parts. The public had the 'white pages' and sat in on stage one. Politically hot matters (as well as personal questions that might genuinely have been prejudiced by public debate) were kept to the confidential 'yellow pages' of the agenda for discussion after the press and public had withdrawn. The members and attendant senior officers took off their jackets, rolled up their sleeves, lit cigarettes and got down to the real business.

The council gradually built up over a period of several years a set of institutions, some of them smart new centres where the public could take their problems, others less visible committees and functions, all intended to mediate its relations with the local people. By 1974, in addition to the ten neighbourhood councils, and *their* advice centres, there was a Consumer Advice Centre, Citizens Advice Bureau, Community Law Centre and Town Planning Advice Centre – all sponsored by the council. The council supported a Community Relations Committee, keeping an eye open for racial strife and funding activities among the black population. The town hall had initiated a 24-hour emergency service. And a new Public Relations Officer was appointed, fresh from the private sector. He was asked to produce a council newspaper and to 'initiate and develop plans for improving contact with the press and public, using all relevant media'.

In the housing field there was the Housing Advice Centre alongside the town hall and regular meetings of the Joint Advisory Housing Committees. A working party on tenant management was set up to see how much further this co-operation might go. The Director of Housing (in 1974) was cautious about extending the policy, but saw two advantages in giving tenants more of a say in the management of their estates. Housing management's twin headaches were 'problem families' and 'vandalism'.

One advantage would be a higher degree of involvement by tenants and therefore a greater responsibility in the tenant to do something for himself and instil a more responsible outlook on life in the less responsible tenants. Second, a better quality of life would result on estates. We can do much as manager, but unless we have full co-operation of tenants we won't achieve much, for instance on

vandalism and destruction. Then they will see it is not as easy to
control as they think it is. They might themselves achieve it better
than us, however.

For the former Housing chairman (1971–73), who was pressing his
own scheme of tenant management, the advantages were as much
punitive as practical. 'People say they want participation and I say
you'll get it whether you like it or not. Participation means decision-
making with responsibility. I have produced this scheme for
housing management. We will say to the tenants "here is the
money, here are the professional people to advise you, now make
your decisions". Then they will meet *our* type of problem. And they
will respond just as we do. Self-management of our estates. It is a
very advanced scheme of participation.' This was the Housing
chairman who was party to the original agreement for the
management of short-life property by the Family Squatters –
presumably within this same philosophy.

All this community-oriented activity, it should be added, whose
implementation rested with many different service departments and
involved much expendidture (£½ million a year on the various
public advice centres alone) was at no time co-ordinated or dealt
with as a distinct community development programme. It was
more in the nature of a style or preoccupation, seldom explicit, that
had come to affect many of the council's activities. For this reason
the documents arising from the appointment of community
workers and the original formula for the neighbourhood councils
scheme have a particular interest. They are among the few papers
that spell out clearly the council's hopes and intentions in
community development.

The first Social Services community worker was employed
on an experimental basis soon after the implementation of the 1970
Act. The co-ordinator of community work was appointed in
February 1973 and soon after his arrival the team of community
workers was brought up to its full strength of eight. The main
emphasis in the co-ordinator's job brief was on his role in liaison
with voluntary organisations and volunteers in the social work

field. He was also, however, required to 'monitor the Social Services aspects' of the neighbourhood councils scheme, and this he did by attending the relevant Sub-Committee. He rejected a proposal from the Deputy Leader for an integration between his community workers and the neighbourhood council operation. He was also to be responsible for 'community development and community work in Social Services' which was interpreted as 'identifying the local needs of each area' and 'ensuring that as far as possible the *community meets its own needs*' (my italics). Community work was defined as stimulating self-help, the partnership of 'community' and local state in the social welfare function. The job description given to his eight community workers was similar. They were 'to *promote the flow of information* concerning community need' into the Directorate to help decide priorities in spending; 'to identify and stimulate *resources from within the community';* and 'to give personal support and advice to social work colleagues and direct to community groups as appropriate in order to stimulate and promote community activity' (my italics).

In the case of the neighbourhood councils, the objectives seemed to be three-fold. One bore on information. The NCs should be 'a method by which the opinions of those who live and work in the borough can be collated and made known to the council so that they may be more fully taken into consideration when determining council policy'.[2] It was hoped they would 'increase communication in both directions between the council and local communities in order that the people of Lambeth may both contribute more fully to the formulation of council policies and be able through their own intervention to help overcome local problems.'[3] In that is implicit the second objective, enlisting community partnership in curing poverty and deprivation. Most important, though, the neighbourhood councils scheme reflected the need for 'extended reproduction' of authority relations in the borough. They wanted to create 'a well informed interest in local government and local affairs' and to help out the councillor as the Labour Party's front man.

Representation of the views of the public has traditionally been the role of the councillor. Increasingly, it is being recognised that with the growth of the Council's services, and the rise in people's expectations from life, traditional channels of communication need to be supplemented by new structures if the views of all the people are to be made known to the Council. There is a growing social awareness among individuals not satisfied by the more traditional outlets for community service. New structures are required which will afford the opportunity to assume a greater personal responsibility in the finding of local solutions to local problems.

It looked very much, therefore, as though the community approach was intended to be strong on just those points that corporate management in Lambeth was weak. It could be a complementary measure. By concentrating on the points of interaction between the council and the population it could have a bearing on the implementation of policies. It could enrich the flows of information about the population into the town hall. And it was also clearly hoped that community development would carry the management initiative into the field of relations between council and public, saving the day for electoral democracy.

The neighbourhood councils scheme

Neighbourhood councils (NCs) are the main focus of this analysis because it is the operation of this scheme that has been most impressive for councillors and officers alike and on it they hold the most clear-cut views. Neighbourhood councils are generally understood to be Lambeth's main contribution to community development practice – everyone had a view on them.

The decision to set up the councils was recorded in the Borough Council Minutes for 14 July 1971. The scheme was given by the Labour leadership into the care of the Finance and General Purposes Committee and placed, with a degree of logic, in the administration of the Public Relations Officer. A staff of five, one of whom was called liaison officer and the remainder neighbourhood council development assistants (I'll call them community development officers (CDOs)) was appointed early on. The liaison officer's main job was to organise the Neighbourhood Council Office in the town hall. Each of the four CDOs was to service a number of individual neighbourhood councils by 'attending all NC meetings and servicing NCs so far as the council is concerned with advice and assistance, including publicity, paper work and, exceptionally, taking minutes.' There was also provision for monetary grants to the NCs, up to about £1,000 a year apiece. The total annual cost of the scheme to the council was about £30,000, of which £8,000 or so came from the Home Office Urban Aid funds.

The first step in approaching the local population was to hold public meetings in five trial areas, to which were invited all known community associations and interest groups in the area and the public at large. The boundaries of the areas were deliberately left vague. There seems to have been no preliminary analysis of economic and social conditions. The areas were not selected on any criterion of deprivation; indeed, the original intention was eventually to have a neighbourhood council for every part of the borough. A good deal of initiative seems to have lain with individual Labour councillors. Much depended upon whether they liked the idea of getting one for their ward. At the first round of meetings the issue was left very open. If local interest were shown, a second meeting would be organised to decide the constitution of neighbourhood council and to form a committee or nucleus of some kind. The council expressed itself open-minded about the structure of management each neighbourhood council should have. Many later felt this to have been a mistake – but for now they simply wanted to get things off the ground.

The council's offer was in the main well received and during the last three months of 1971 six neighbourhood councils were established. By 1974 there were ten. They varied a good deal in their internal structure. Most started out having a fairly large committee elected at public meeting. Sometimes this was called the 'council'. None actually held elections on the lines of borough council elections with a poll involving the whole electoral register.[4] Some, North Lambeth and Vassall for instance, started off as a group of individuals elected at a public meeting and later went over to a representative system whereby tenants associations, street groups and other local organisations in the area sent delegates to a federal committee.[5]

The largest area for a neighbourhood council was that of South Lambeth, which covered 20,000 population. Among the smallest were Josephine Avenue NC and Rommany NC, covering districts with no more than 5,000 people apiece. Size of area did not necessarily correlate with size and activity of membership, however. South Lambeth, though large, was one of the more sleepy, while Josephine Avenue, on a rather more limited range of issues ('street lighting, refuse collection nuisance and the layout of local open space'), was very active. Rommany covered a compulsory purchase order area, scheduled for redevelopment in the late seventies and aimed to negotiate the best deal for local people in the ensuing blight and dispersal. Two of the smaller NCs covered districts mainly comprised in a council 'general improvement area' and much of their attention was focused on the council's rehabilitation and environmental improvement schemes. They became the mechanism for participation in those plans. Birkbeck NC for instance put forward an alternative traffic scheme and won the council's admiration by presenting 'the findings of a detailed and professionally executed door to door survey to a public meeting attended by the council'. They sent in a report which they hoped would 'constitute a reasoned basis for discussion and reappraisal' by the council.

King's Acre and North Lambeth NCs were both born with plenty of help from the midwife, in the form of the local Labour Party. King's Acre was actually constituted as a result of a request from the ward councillors – theirs was a marginal ward with a relatively healthy Labour Party. The Leader (in interview) pointed to King's Acre as a notably successful neighbourhood council.

North Lambeth was encouraged in its early days by the Labour Whip on the council, together with one or two other influential Labour councillors from the neighbourhood. Its leading light was a vicar, the husband of a councillor. It was seen by the CD officer as an attempt to be an umbrella group, welding together the better-off people of its area (who were also the activists in the Labour Party) with the poorer working class in the local population. 'On the one hand there were the members who had a professional, albeit genuine, interest in the functions of the NC,' he wrote in his report, 'as architects, local clergy, social workers, etc., and on the other local tenants who felt they had, through bad housing and lack of amenities, suffered through neglect on the part of the local authorities and were willing to fight to bring this to the attention of the authorities and gain improvements.' As a result there was much division and strain in the life of this neighbourhood council. But the CD personnel were a strong influence upon it, 'The Social Services Community Worker practically runs their advice centre.' It was felt to be going about things the right way.

Most neighbourhood councils were, by 1974, satisfying the council's expectations. They kept the council on its toes without treading on them too often. Two neighbourhood councils are worth considering in more detail, because they represent the points at which for different interests within the town hall the management returns in community development began to be outweighed by political discomfort.

Vassall went well beyond most NCs in the degree of its organisation and enthusiasm. Its first chairman was, again, a vicar – but he was quickly succeeded by a school teacher. The secretary was an architect teaching in a polytechnic. They had already come to blows with the council as members of a tenants' association pressing the interests of the former residents of the Minet Estate which had been bought out by the council. Large areas of Vassall ward were undergoing the painfully slow and disruptive process of demolition and redevelopment. Much of the area was rubble; and for those remaining behind in half-empty streets, waiting their turn to go, life was uncertain and miserable.

The NC quickly crossed swords with the bureaucracy. The Housing Director (1972–74) refused to allow one of his officers to keep a public meeting appointment with the NC. 'There was uproar,' said the chairman. Eventually both the Director of Housing and the Director of Development had to turn up in person to a NC meeting. They wanted to tape record the proceedings; the NC refused to allow this; there was much acrimony. The NC grew stronger, organising a network of tenant and street groups in the ward. It asked the council to knock down three empty houses to make space for a play site for the dismal Cowley estate. The council stalled for a year. The NC then organised a noisy demonstration, women and children made a scene at the town hall, and the council gave them their playspace. In all this the CD officer responsible for Vassall kept a low profile in the town hall and gave a good deal of practical support to the organisers.

We saw in Chapter 3 the way in which Vassall NC made and publicised a survey of the appalling housing situation in the ward and set up its own squatting group. The Vassall squatting organisers were, however, very 'reasonable' in their approach to the council, continually asked for recognition and co-operation, and when the 'licensing' scheme was introduced they were the only group in the borough prepared to accept it. (They later changed their mind.)

While the short-life housing issue did touch some councillors on the raw, Vassall NC did not seem more than momentarily to forfeit the approval of most elected members. It was generally accounted a 'very successful' neighbourhood council, it had shown 'initiative'. Many councillors were happy enough to see the big guns on the officer side spiked by the activists. For the officers, however, Vassall had gone too far.

The officers' dislike for Vassall, however, in no way matched the venom they felt against Angell neighbourhood council. This was one NC which was universally condemned by officers and members alike. The reason for this was the qualitatively different nature of its organisation and the demands it gave rise to. The organising nucleus of its NC was a group of private tenants. Their political action was developed from experience as students in and after 1968, so they brought to these housing struggles a suspicion of hierarchy and bureaucracy, both in the state institutions and in political parties. Their first-hand experience was of sit-ins and other forms of direct action. Angell's distinguishing characteristic among the NCs as a whole was that it placed itself firmly outside the ambit of electoral representative democracy. It refused to collaborate with elected members. 'Councillors are elected to power, which means taking something away from the community. They get sustenance from a radical party locally, like Norwood, but it is a machine they dust down and roll over the people at election time. A good councillor will either be trodden down and discarded, or he'll change and go on up to higher things,' said one of Angell NC organisers.

In Angell's news-sheet were systematically published extracts from confidential council papers coming into the NC's hands, and editorials analysed the structural economic reasons for local distress in a way which set the neighbourhood council apart from the others in the scheme. The organising group had developed 'a commitment to politics at the level of the base group, where an understanding and collective action could develop out of people's experience and where organisation could be informal and genuinely democratic' (interview). The interaction of these two sets of experience: of student politics and of the life of council tenants on poor estates, produced for a couple of years a kind of involvement of ordinary people that traditional, more elitist, tenants' associations had been quite unable to generate.

Lilford Estate affords an example. It is an old estate of 180 tenancies in Angell ward, formerly belonging to the GLC. It is bleak, minimal housing provision, deeply depressing especially for the many mothers of young children living there. There was no tenants association on Lilford until 1972. At that point a small group of men and women got together, about the time of the Housing Finance Act, and formed a tenants association which became one of the base groups of the new neighbourhood council. They and others in the NC decided not to fight the Housing Finance Act through lobbying MPs alongside the local Labour Party, since they believed (rightly as it happened) that a Labour sell-out was inevitable. Instead they would get one step ahead and plan to overstrain the appeals machinery in order to hinder actual implementation of the rent rises that would follow the Act. When the first round of increases (55p across the board) was announced in letters to tenants in August 1972, 90 per cent of the Lilford tenants sent letters objecting. One-third withheld the increase, some paying it into an emergency fund opened by the tenants association. They arranged to go in company to pay their rent so as to avoid intimidation. The second stage of implementation of the Act began with letters to tenants in February 1973, outlining proposed rent increases up to 1975. Again, 83 per cent of the tenants wrote to the council objecting. In fact, of the 946 letters of objection received by the council from the entire borough 150 came from this one little estate. All the letters needed personal replies. Part of the intention of the tenants association had been to cost the council time and trouble.

A second issue taken up by Lilford TA was that of transfers. There were old people in top flats needing ground floor flats. There were people with many children in small flats and retired couples in large flats. The council was unresponsive to requests for transfers, even within the estate. Angell NC and the tenants association began to see that what was needed was a more flexible system whereby parents could hand tenancies to children, husbands to wives, etc. They proposed two transfers to the council who failed to endorse them. Then the TA took things into their own hands and carried out some transfers independently. They started a 'swop shop' in the news-sheet. The council quickly concurred in this *fait accompli*. A secondary effect was speedier response by the council to requests for repairs.

The left-wing Vice-Chairman of the Housing Committee (1971–73), mentioned previously in connection with his promotion of official squatting, was a Housing Finance Act non-implementer. He had promised Lilford tenants that no one would be victimised for withholding the increase. When he resigned his housing office in 1973 Lilford called the Chairman of Housing (1973–74) to a meeting and asked for his assurance, in turn, on this point. When he refused to give it, angry scenes ensued and an aggressive article appeared in the news-sheet. This and other incidents contributed to his downfall and replacement after the 1974 council elections.

It was in Angell ward that council tenants pioneered the use of Section 99 of the Public Health Act 1936 to take the council to court as a slum landlord and require it to carry out repairs on council houses. Trial cases were raised concerning houses in Flaxman and Belinda Roads, where tenants were suffering blocked pipes, falling plaster, rotten floorboards, leaking roofs, broken window frames and sashcords, crumbling brickwork and faulty guttering. The council tended, of course, to prefer quickly to set about repairs than to have to face a court case. This kind of legal action became possible through the formation of the Public Health Inspectors London Action Group (an organisation of qualified PHIs who were prepared to act outside their terms of employment by the local state) and of the Community Law Centre in Brixton, sponsored incidentally by the council as part of its community approach. The Law Centre was able to put lawyers, familiar with court procedure, at the service of housing groups. The law courts, or threat of legal action, was also used in Lambeth to get injunctions on private landlords to repair and to force the council in its turn to pursue its legal obligation to carry out the work where landlords failed. A year or two later successful court cases were brought to obtain 'home loss payments' from the council for families being decanted for purposes of rehabilitation – an important and expensive precedent for the council.

The way in which Angell NC turned the council's own community weapons against it, and its extreme scepticism of all councillors, led to much bad feeling in the Labour Group. The Chairman of Housing (1973–74) said in interview, 'Some neighbourhood councils are responsible and excellent; some are irresponsible and unsuccessful; Angell has been a total failure.' The secretary of their constituency Labour Party was less restrained: 'Angell – I'd shoot the lot,' he said.

Trouble at the interface

The connecting link between the neighbourhood councils and the council itself was a new sub-committee of Finance and General

Purposes Committee called the Neighbourhood Councils Sub-Committee. The drama surrounding it reveals the essentially delicate nature of community development for both the authority and activist groups. At the outset all seemed ship-shape. The Sub-Committee had nine councillor members and the following delegated powers:

> To implement the Council's policy in relation to the neighbourhood councils, to keep such policy under review and to make any necessary recommendations thereon from time to time to the Finance and General Purposes Committee and to deal with requests for the appointment of Council representatives in connection with neighbourhood councils. It is authorised to deal with applications for financial and other assistance from neighbourhood councils within the provisions approved by the Council.

The sub-committee was chaired by the deputy leader (1971–74), the originator and promoter of the neighbourhood councils scheme. At the second meeting, representatives of the neighbourhood councils were invited to attend 'with the privilege of participation in the proceedings'. At the following meeting, the Sub-Committee members decided to go further and give representatives 'the right to speak and vote on all agenda items, on the basis of separate voting by council and neighbourhood council sides'. The idea was that if items on the agenda were approved by both sides, the reports would go up to the relevant main committee of council with a recommendation for action. If approved by one side and rejected by the other, they would be passed up for information only. This was an ingenious arrangement – unprecedented in fact. It seems to have originated with the deputy leader and have been supported by other members of the sub-committee. Later it caused trouble, as we shall see.

Quite apart from the contact that a number of neighbourhood councils had through their ward councillors with the town hall, they all had regular contact with the council and with each other through the meetings of this sub-committee, where they came once every six weeks and sat alongside the nine council members.

Debate on the sub-committee was increasingly energetic as time went by, and often led to bitterness. From dealing with constitutional and management problems of neighbourhood councils it quickly moved on to discussions of substantive matters raised by the neighbourhood councils, covering many aspects of council policy and bearing on many committees' business, especially that of Housing and of Development. 'The NCs used it as a platform for stating their point of view to councillors and officers and to force a vote sometimes on certain issues which had quite an embarrassing effect on the council,' said the chairman of Vassall NC. For this reason, and because the items were among the most contentious on council agendas, many senior officers had to be present at the chairman's call-over and often felt it necessary to stay on and hear out the meetings in case their department came under attack. It was, constitutionally, an unusual state of affairs. Besides, since the Sub-Committee was able to lodge any item passing through their own agenda onto the public part of any council main committee agenda, anything that the press failed to pick up at Sub-Committee they usually caught second time round at the main committee.

In early 1973 the council's senior officers reacted. The rejuvenation of political life had never been their priority: they had always seen the neighbourhood councils scheme as the members' affair. Indeed (the NC liaison officer reported), officers declined to take part in the forward planning for neighbourhood council policy in 1973–74 and made it clear that they considered that to be an issue for members. Theoretically, perhaps, they should have been interested in constructive criticism and helpful attempts to co-operate in improving urban management. The neighbourhood councils pointed over and again to the two main weaknesses in the council's management system: planning and housing. To those councillors able to take a high-level view of community develop-ment it was possible to see that this was exactly the function that, if it were to serve the local state well, it would perform. It should show up the weak spots in the management system in such a way that the overall system might correct them – even offering some of the means. But, being human (notwithstanding the suspicions of some NCs), the Directors of these two particular departments and some others that were shown up by the debates on the sub-committee, were not prone to take this olympian and detached view of the good of the whole system. They felt personally threatened.

The Chief Executive and Directors' Board submitted a report to a special meeting of the Policy Committee. In the report the directors made certain complaints and recommendations in regard to the sub-committee. They complained, first, that the neighbourhood councils were creating too much work, too many meetings and too many requests for information. The Director of Administrative and Legal Services (under whose remit the neighbourhood councils fell) submitted 'a report which stressed the exorbitant amount of his officers' time which had to be spent in circulating minutes and publicity material for neighbourhood councils, and which specified that there would be "visiting hours" at the town hall for neighbourhood council members in future, viz. 8.45 a.m. to 10.00 a.m. and 2.00 p.m. to 3.00 p.m. Some seven reports had been submitted for the agenda by neighbourhood councils in wholly insufficient time to enable the officers to consider them, many critical of the council's administration.'[6] The officers also complained that proposals coming into committee through the sub-committee evaded the corporate decision process, they were 'not necessarily informed of the wider context of the relevant established programmes and priorities of the council'.

It was clear too that the new procedure incurred by the existence of neighbourhood councils was obscuring the normal division of labour between officers and members to which officers were accustomed: officers were being called (at all too short notice, what is more) to report on items being placed on main committee agendas by the sub-committee and thus to comment on proposals that had already had the agreement of some elected members. This they felt was improper, unconstitutional. They expressed resentment at the way NC activities cut across their own, often statutory and long-standing, 'participation' exercises with the public. They were distressed by the loss of protocol and neglect of hierarchy when NCs demanded access to officers 'at all levels'. And most feelingly, they expressed concern that they and their staff were being 'subjected to critical and even discourteous, hostile and slanderous remarks when they attended NC meetings and this was particularly unjust when they have given up their free time to assist the NCs by their presence.'[7]

The hard feelings of the senior officers were discussed at Policy Comittee. The progress and the effects of the NC's scheme now came under review. The NC's main supporter, the deputy leader and chairman of their sub-committee, defended his scheme. He protested 'there is a feeling abroad that community participation is all very well so long as the community does what the council expects it to do. That was never a principle embodied in the original concept of neighbourhood councils and I trust it can be got rid of now once and for all.' He urged 'the need to key the demands of the neighbourhood councils into the committee system of local government'. He reminded Policy Committee that 'the great mass of people have never been encouraged by any of the major parties to enter into a continuing debate on the policy adopted by the representatives of the people at any level. . . . There is no reason,' he said, 'why the critical aspect of neighbourhood councils should not be usefully utilised for the benefit both of the community and the council. What they are providing within their criticisms is a unique grassroots knowledge of the problems of Lambeth and understanding those problems and the way in which they affect our local community is a first step to enabling this council to solve them.'[8] He would like to see neighbourhood councils developed as the sole or primary channel of communications between the community in the area which they serve. It is possible to recognise now, in the light of the foregoing discussion of systems theory, that what the deputy leader had in mind was a progressive and effective adaptation of urban management but one which was some way in advance of those who had to implement it.

There was never any question in Labour group, even now, of going back on the neighbourhood scheme as a whole. Public uproar would certainly follow. Besides, it was clear by now that the scheme did have certain uses. There were, however, doubters among the elected members, some of whom felt that the scheme was turning out to the detriment of the individual councillor and his ward role. Some NCs were causing members to 'play second fiddle', by increasing the direct interaction between local groups and officers. Neighbourhood councils were acting as 'surrogate councillors'. It was wrong to suppose that individuals in the community were free to choose whomsoever they liked to represent their interests to the council: the constitutionally elected person was the only valid representative.

The NCs had, from the start, been ordained into a 'special relationship' with the council. It resided in the arrangement by which they received money from the council, had access to council information by means of their support staff, the CD officers; and had their own sub-committee. These things set them apart from ordinary outside groups. This 'special relationship' had to go. Neighbourhood councils should be cut off from the council. If they wanted to get items considered by council committees they should be required to go through ward councillors, their own parent directorate, and the chairmen of committees, just as other ordinary community groups would have to do. They should be able to send representatives to listen from the public gallery, without special privilege and be allowed to speak only at the discretion of the committee, like everyone else.[9]

A compromise was put forward by the Chairman of Finance (1971–74) and supported by one or two others, including the Deputy Leader. Neighbourhood councils should be given a new constitution, should be required to hold proper elections and become fully representative and responsible bodies. The 'special relationship' should continue. The sub-committee should remain in existence but NCs should have no voting powers on it. Everyone agreed that the NCs should be briefed to mind their own business in future, concentrating their attention more onto the development of community life in their areas and less onto council policy.

Labour group then debated the question. The voting was close. Against the advice of its chairman they decided to disband the sub-committee. Nothing more was said about formal and mandatory constitutions for the NCs. A brief announcement reached the NCs from the Labour Whip. It simply said that the sub-committee was being closed because group wished to 'simplify the procedure' by enabling NCs to table items direct onto main committee agendas, and so 'expedite their consideration'.[10] The neighbourhood councils were almost all embittered by the decision. They nonetheless continued in existence and adapted their approach. Vassall and Angell which had been the most political in their approach, using the Sub-Committee to challenge the council, suffered more than others by the new practice. Angell became less active. Vassall sought a closer relationship with ward councillors after the 1974 elections.

What were the CD officers' feelings at this point in time? In the same way that the new professionals, the corporate planning staff, were able to voice the philosophy behind corporate management and planning in Lambeth, this second group of newcomers, also struggling towards a professional identity, expressed the hopes of 'progressive' officials for community development. Their public view was that NCs should play an active part in council management – similar to the 'social planning' role discussed in Chapter 4. Privately several believed that a measure of militancy would have a good effect on this social planning process. In May 1974 after the closure of the Sub-Committee, they wrote of their feeling that the council, although it had espoused the idea of community development, was not giving it the support it needed if it was to have a real effect on council policy. They complained that the council was not living up to the 'special relationship' that had been promised. 'It has become apparent that there is considerable "statutory reluctance" resulting in problems of *accommodating the neighbourhood councils into the council structure and administration,'* they wrote (my italics). 'In Lambeth, this has so far prevented the NCs from becoming actively engaged in local government.' They wanted the NCs to be more integrated with the town hall. They wanted a renewed commitment and a clearer agreement about purpose. 'It is reasonable to expect that most NCs will favour a role that incorporates some aspect of liaison between council and community, a body that can co-ordinate opinion and resources beyond the scope . . . of the localised community action group.' They asked for a *closer link with ward councillors* and for quarterly meetings; more discussion by officers with the NCs of council business concerning their areas; they wanted to make a *regular and formal input to policy*.[11]

Balance of advantage

What can we conclude about these experiences and their meaning for the decision-makers in the local state and for the local working-class population? The management gains offered by the community approach at any level of intensity bring with them costs and dangers for the local state. In Lambeth the balance of advantage seemed to hinge around a number of issues. One significant factor was the degree of isolation or solidarity achieved by local groups. A second was their attitude to the Labour Party and electoral democracy. A third was the internal structure of the groups. Finally, and more important than the rest, much hinged on the nature of the mechanism that linked them to the council. I'll discuss these factors briefly in that order.

There was no doubt that one of the ideas behind the neighbourhood council's scheme was that of grouping local associations in a way that matched to a modest degree the council's own integrated structure and so enabled transactions to take place that were useful and meaningful in the council's terms. 'Neighbourhood councils have a structural role in the community, stimulating a corporate approach by the community, getting people together . . . they should be there as liaison between council and government bodies on the one hand and the community on the other, feeding information across,' said the former Leader (1971–73). Nonetheless it was important for the council to get the corporate approach on the community side at the right scale. A corporate approach within a neighbourhood seems (all other things being equal) to be something the council can see as useful. It did not want and could not manage a borough-wide corporate approach of the kind that was emerging in Lambeth through the meetings of the neighbourhood councils. It made the NCs seem almost as legitimate an expression of public opinion as the council itself. It was particularly hazardous for the council since the NCs felt they experienced similar abuses by the council. 'The idea of them banding together, other than to compare notes, is a negation of their role. They are meant to be local,' said the Chairman of Finance. The NCs did get together, many of them, with each other and with squatters and residents of the 'half-way houses' for the homeless, in an all-Lambeth campaign against the council's housing policies in the spring of 1974. But the solidarity could have gone much further than it did – and been more challenging to the council. There was little attempt, for instance, to form a front with local union branches, not even with those unions representing council workers.

Secondly, there arises the question of the attitude of the NCs to local electoral democracy and the Labour Party. NCs that worked co-operatively with members were appreciated and congratulated. Vassall for instance behaved 'responsibly' in inviting candidates from all the political parties to publish statements in their news-sheet before the election. This was compared favourably with Angell, who simply ran a long feature in *their* news-sheet on why it was better not to be ballot-fodder at all. When NCs stepped outside the party political frame of reference, as Angell did, choosing to work on issues beyond the scope of the council's powers, either because of economic constraints or the internal disarray of its administration, that marked a cut-off point for the Labour group's interest.

The question of the internal structure of the neighbourhood councils was under continual discussion among councillors. Many felt that it had been a mistake that the council had not laid down a constitution for neighbourhood councils. 'If you give them ratepayers' money they should be accountable and visible,' said a councillor, summing up the general attitude. A proper committee structure, with proper election of secretary, treasurer and chairman, was held to be vital. As to whether they should be, as some councillors wanted, 'a mini-federation of tenants and other associations', or directly elected by the electoral roll or at a public meeting, was an open question. Some felt they should be forced to be strictly representative and answerable to the public as a whole in their area; others felt that the legitimacy this would confer on NCs would be even *more* of a direct threat to the ward councillor. One of the causes of resentment against Angell and one of the reasons, in the eyes of its organisers, for that NC's success in mobilising action in support of working class interests was that it had evolved an internal structure that included many of the ordinary members in activity, with key roles such as secretary and chairman rotating or absent. The NC activists had learned from the experience of other active groups in Lambeth that the council is capable of co-opting any leadership that becomes apparent, dealing with the committee at the expense of the members.

Finally, the point around which most heated dispute arose was the design of the linking mechanism between the NCs and the town hall. The sub-committee was affording militants a direct inlet to the decision-makers, penetrating under the guard of the committee system and the directorates. That is why it was disbanded and why the leader, who was happy enough for the development of the NCs to continue, 'one or two more anyway', was concentrating on the re-design of the interface between the NCs and the town hall. He favoured sending the CD officers out to be on the payroll of the grant-aided NCs, and keeping the liaison officer only in the town hall.

It is interesting to note that this solution would have given the liaison officer something of the same role as the co-ordinator of community work in the Directorate of Social Services. This had proved a trouble-free design for the council. In spite of the existence in the community work team of a number of conflict-prone community workers, disruption had been kept to a level below which it was felt to need review by members. Certainly the leader was tolerant. 'It's annoying sometimes. Senior officers complain about them bitterly. But you have to live with it. It's best to turn a blind eye to some of these things.' It may be clear now why they were not more disruptive than they were. The community workers in the field were isolated from each other in their area teams, unlike the NCs and their CDOs who met in the Neighbourhood Councils Office in the town hall and in the sub-committee. For community workers there was no such combining of viewpoints. They were integrated into one of the service departments and their input into the political system of 'community need', or disruption, whichever way it was seen, normally stopped within this department. At most it reached the Social Services Committee – and could be ignored without comeback. The community workers reported primarily to the area social work superiors whose tendency was to impress a strongly case-work identity on their work. The co-ordinator was isolated within the council structure, isolated even within Social Services, and had no structural link with members and little individual contact with them.

The community workers themselves sensed these weaknesses in their position and proposed a number of changes.[12] First, they wanted it recognised that their work would be concerned, like that of the CDOs, with policy fields other than Social Services. It should concern the *whole work of the council*. (They wanted, in other words, to enter the field that mainly caused problems for the local working class: housing and planning.) Second, they asked for facilities for a *co-ordinated* community work team, with its own office and secretarial support. They wanted to develop, they wrote, a picture of need in the borough as a whole. Third, they wanted the status that would enable them to get information freely from other departments and to act across departmental boundaries. The co-ordinator, who preferred his community-care orientation, rejected this proposal, no doubt with the happy support of senior officers.

It is interesting to speculate whether the council might not, in fact, have pulled some management advantage out of encouraging its community workers to open up more active working links between Social Services, Housing, Planning and other departments. An astute Chief Executive might have seen in these cross-connections just the kind of low-level integrative mechanism lacking in his hierarchical structure. In the same way we should not necessarily see the rather distant relationship between the council and the NCs, adopted as a quiet life solution after 1974, as a clear-cut gain for the council. Take the question of squatting. Several NCs (in addition to Vassall) had asked for squatting agreements with the council. Such was its internal disarray that the Housing Directorate had been unable to respond to such offers of participation in the use of short-life housing. Indeed it had even felt unable to maintain its original partnership with the Family Squatters. But to co-operate in this way with the NCs might well have enabled the council to prevent the squatting situation escalating as it did and to hold the authority relation, at least for a while, in better shape.

The experience in Lambeth is interesting for its dynamic, the way it unfolded over three or four years. These factors we've been discussing can be seen as scales – there is a possible range from less to greater formality of structure; less to greater contact between groups and council and so on. The point on these various scales at which advantage is felt to tip from the local state to the local working class, or from the working class to the state, is continually shifting. Since 1968 the shift had been steadily towards a higher level of interaction: until the cut-off point of the closure of the Sub-Committee. We saw parallel developments in community work nationally – which shifted from social pathology, through social planning to the conflict method. In 1974, having learned how to survive and handle the activism of neighbourhood councils, both officers and councillors must have been satisfied with their new robustness. They had travelled far from the inexperience and discomfiture of the early days of public participation. In the same way many people in the borough had woken up to a new sense of their own power.

6. The new terrain of class struggle

Lambeth's experience was shared by many other urban councils. The local authority made efforts to respond to the urging of the government and to the dictates of their own common sense by modernising their management systems. Tighter personnel management, aimed to improve productivity in time of an expanding local government workforce, assisted in rationalisation in time of cutback. New techniques of financial planning were applied first to a growing budget, later in a period of restraint, finally after 1974 to devising cuts in expenditure. But stronger management in the town hall could not, in the brightest economic circumstances let alone in crisis, respond to the needs of an urban working class whose distress was caused mainly by factors well beyond the council's control. On matters where local people felt that the state was failing to provide essential services, particularly housing, to an adequate standard they attacked the council, often using in these struggles the participatory and 'community' support mechanisms offered by the council itself. It now remains to pull together the question of active struggles of this kind and link it to the theoretical framework within which this story is elaborated.

In this final chapter I look first at the category of '*community action*' and the weaknesses that experience has shown it to hold; and demonstrate on the contrary the strengths of strategies for collective action that are developing around the concept of *reproduction*. Taking the class relationships that the idea of reproduction makes possible I then go on to look at the three places where such action is developing: the point of *collective reproduction** (where we are 'clients' of state 'services'); the point of *employment in*

* See footnote on p.64.

reproduction (where we are the workforce of the local state); and the point of *privatised reproduction* (our family life).

'Community' belongs to capital

The phrase that has come to be used to describe almost any collective action going on outside the workplace is 'community action'. It rings with implausibility. Why? All through this discussion I've avoided the term, only using the word 'community' where the state has chosen to use it. This was for a reason. It is not the activity, so much as the CATEGORY that needs questioning. It is not just a question of using or not using a form of expression, but of *thinking* with it. I'll suggest four reasons – three of which are fundamental and one tactical. All are related.

First, to think in terms of community action places struggle on ground prepared, over a long historical period, by the state. It takes a shape that is expected, anticipated and even proposed by the state. In a sense (to use an ecological metaphor) the state is the environment that offers a vacant 'niche', a milieu that will reward and foster a certain kind of behaviour, and the fledgling initiatives of struggle step in to fill it.

The local electoral representative system has been, since its inception, based on territorial definition of interest group. The local councillor represents the ward, wards are grouped into constituencies, constituencies into boroughs. More recently the local services of councils, too, have decentralised themselves, partially, into area teams and area offices, again using territory as the basis for this organisation. In recent years, and in some boroughs, not only is there a ward councillor and an area housing manager and several other officials on the spot to relate to whatever 'community' may arise – there is a community worker too. They have even revamped the local bobby into the community policeman. When territorial working class community groups arise there is a set of officers and councillors, in a sense waiting for them, to, whom the community group is of vital relevance and who have their own preconceptions which they will bring to bear on its activities.

One effect of the presence of a ward councillor and a community worker in the territory is to encourage the idea that problems arise in 'officialdom' – because this is something that they both know something about and are ready to tackle. 'The expression that workers and peasants initially give to their discontent is generally diffuse and fragmentary and it often moves into a simple anti-authoritarianism such as "dislike of officialdom" – the only form in which the state is perceived.'[1] If discontent is addressed against the local bureaucracy and the top politicians (the Labour leadership) that join with them in urban management, the answer is too easily seen as lying with the ward councillor of left-wing or populist sympathies. And this, as I'll suggest below, has its dangers for collective action.

The second, related, argument against relying on a concept of 'community action' is that it has been closely connected since its rise to popularity in the late sixties with consumer protection. It tends to cast us in the role of consumers (of capital's products and the state's services), a position that is economically and politically weak. What has been called community action has been rationalised as something that arises NOT from capitalism itself, but from some of the more unfortunate but curable effects of the current stage of technological development. 'We all suffer at the hands of large and insensitive organisations and we are all emotionally stunted by the amorphous uniformity of the cosmopolitan culture to which we belong' – that is the way it is commonly put.[2] Selma James put her finger on what is happening: 'we have inherited a distorted and reformist concept of capital itself as a series of things which we struggle to plan, control or manage, rather than as a social relation which we struggle to destroy.'[3] Community action points not to deficiencies in the mode of production but in the products: the goods or services.

Third, community action is all too often defined as classless. In common usage it is a populist formulation, open to all classes, groups and interests. Where it *is* defined to exclude 'the middle class' it is nonetheless normally focused not on the working class as such but on 'the deprived', 'the poor' or even the 'poor-poor'. In other words, it bites off what the Victorians called the residuum, the problem-fraction of the people, and distinguishes it from the 'real' working class. This splintering is reflected in the bourgeois ideology of pluralism and participatory democracy, the essence of which is that no one group in society should be too *big*. There is in the idea of community action the idea of smallness up against bigness. We are asked to think of the David of one small council estate taking on the Goliath of the town hall. 'Small is beautiful.' It is an image which totally rules out the reality of class struggle, in which huge and powerful forces are ranged against each other, not momentarily, but over centuries. It imposes blinkers which stop one working class group looking to another with similar problems as its natural ally and leads to a situation where groups in neighbourhood territories struggle in competition for the limited resources offered them – a situation often exploited by a local council.

Bernard Greaves,[4] an enthusiast of community action, illustrates this close link between territorial organisations and classlessness. He describes a universal movement, developing as its main power-base residential neighbourhood communities. Among their 'crucial assets' is the following. 'They are socially unifying. Taking over existing power structures is inevitably divisive and leads to such destructive and dangerous concepts as the class war. Building alternative communities enables people of different backgrounds, whether of class, income, employment or whatever, to enter into new relationships on a basis of co-operation deriving from the discovery of a sense of common identity.' The rhetoric of community action here is indistinguishable from the state's own community package. The function of such community action is the maintenance of membership in a capitalist social formation, class positions firmly held though culturally muted.

The fourth (tactical) point is essentially an illustration of the first. The national political parties are now using community action and community politics for competitive *electoral* purposes. Even the Communist Party recognises its political uses. 'Community Groups Fill Gaping Vacuum' (wrote Dave Cook, national election agent of the CP). 'The growth of community action is very much in line with the perspectives outlined in the CP programme. Greater participation by Communists and others on the left is necessary to ensure that community action draws closer to traditional working class organisation.'[5] It is interesting to note that the CP was included with the three bigger national parties in the invitation by the Department of the Environment to comment on the Neighbourhood Councils scheme.

The Liberals too adopted 'community politics' as a shot in the arm for the Party after a crushing electoral defeat in 1970. At the next Party conference a resolution was put forward by Young Liberals that the Party see its role as helping 'organise people in communities to take and use power'. Failing any other new idea to shore up the Party in its collapse, or even of any concerted opposition to this one, the resolution was accepted and grassroots goings-on became a plank in the Party's platform . . . to the rage of Tories and Labour alike who called it mindless opportunism and marketing technique. It led the Liberals to success in Liverpool Corporation and to big votes in Manchester and other urban areas.

If 'community action', then, is not a helpful concept to describe working class struggle outside the job situation, what is? There have been attempts to place it in a historical situation going back to the Diggers and Levellers of the bourgeois revolution of the seventeenth century, to Tom Paine and to Bakunin and the anarchists.[6] This doesn't get us much further. It identifies these struggles with a particular libertarian tendency in revolutionary socialism. There is an important insistence on experience and autonomy; on 'prefigurative' struggle, including the ends among the means of action; a rejection of leadership and of the imposition of theoretical demands that don't spring from day-to-day working class understanding. It is true that Big Flame and many smaller political groups working 'in the community' do reflect this tradition. But such a definition says more about the style of community struggles than about their content or context.

Since many of the issues arising in communities arise in the state services, there is a case for defining our action as anti-state struggles. But to do so deflects attention away from the mode of production, which is the real cause of exploitation. It tends to give the state too much importance and apparent detachment from the economic base.

Shifting the emphasis to reproduction

What then? There is no similar catch phrase. I believe we have to rely clearly and simply on the analysis of the local state that we are attempting; we have to see that what we are involved in is *struggle in the field of capitalist reproduction*. We have to recognise that alongside struggle at the point of production, in the mines and factories, there is struggle at the point of reproduction, in schools, on housing estates, in the street, in the family.

This definition is a strong one because it immediately brings into the field of action, alongside 'client' action by residents on housing, patients' action on health services, etc., the *workers employed by the state*, both professional and manual. Furthermore, it identifies the significance of the action of *women in the home*, in privatised reproduction.

A number of other insights follow. Now we see the inseparable nature of production and reproduction in capitalism we can also see the inseparability of industrial struggle and action over reproductive services such as housing. It also shows us ways of making the connections that are so badly needed between the two. Even the male worker now recognises that, when he went home with his wage packet formerly he was expected to 'reproduce' his own labour power with it – pay his rent, pay his doctor, insure himself through his provident fund. If now the state takes on some of these responsibilities, it is because he has established this right through struggle. The social services have become an intrinsic part of his wage: the social wage. In part, too, the cost of them has been recouped by the state in the increased tax and insurance contributions that he pays. Struggles around housing or benefits or schools are *economic*, as well as 'merely' political. Those things too must be protected against the erosions of inflation and the pressure of profit. In Lambeth, as we saw, the industrial base is declining and the position of organised labour is weak – but there are nonetheless active unions in construction, rail transport and other kinds of work and a Trades Council that could support or engage in reproduction as well as production struggles in that area.

Second, it underpins changes in the nature of workplace struggles too. These are coming to be extended to take account not just of wages and conditions but of that part of life where reproduction goes on – life at home. Working mothers are never likely to make the mistake of seeing higher pay as the only, or even the main, demand. For them the most important thing is that the conditions of paid work respond, when necessary, to the needs of children, to take account of sickness and so on. It will force onto the agenda of workplace action the reproductive issues that should be there. An example for instance is agency work by temporary secretaries and agency nurses. Traditional workers' action resists the introduction of agency staff into a firm or institution because their presence weakens the position of employees. Yet these agency staff are often working mothers who are in this form of employment because their reproductive job at home means they *need* flexible hours and terms of work that employers themselves will not provide. What they do *not* need is to be employed in a structure that causes them to compete with organised labour: it is employers alone who benefit from that. Recognition of an issue like this can extend workplace struggle to a wider solidarity.

On the other hand, taking the theme of reproduction as a starting point enables us to see that production is not the only place of valid struggle. There is a tradition in marxism that distinguishes the economic from the political. The economic is singled out as the sphere of struggle: the shop floor of manufacturing and extractive industry is where the big guns are. Community activists have felt defeated on account of the very terrain on which they stand. 'The most fundamental weakness was built into the very nature of community-based struggle,' concluded the Camden Community Workshop in 1972.[7]

There are clearly definable and quickly experienced limits, built into the situation of localised neighbourhood organising. As a residence-based group the Workshop doesn't face the original source of poverty and powerlessness. The organising is away from the job, the factory, production, where the primary contradiction between wage-labour and capital is located; the contradictions the Workshop seeks to bring to the surface are secondary ones: in housing, education, play, health and social security. The organising is not within production but within the area of distribution, not where people work but where they reside.

The services of the welfare state need not be seen as mere distribution – things which matter to us but not to capital. It is clear that capital itself needs the labour force to be reproduced and above all needs our acceptance of capitalism to be reproduced. The whole social formation depends upon it. To the extent that these functions fail, capitalism is threatened. We do not have to see this whole massive build-up in state expenditure only as a burden on capital. Costly it may be but 'more and more it is a necessary precondition of private capital accumulation'.[8] When such expenditure is cut by the state, as in 1975 and 1976, it is under pressure of a real crisis for capital, when restoring the rate of profit or investment becomes an imperative. To know that the work of the woman in the family and the state worker are indirectly productive of surplus value, that they build rather than diminish private profit, encourages the search for ways of reorganising our domestic labour to suit our own political and social needs.

Is it true, besides, that in production one is 'facing the original source of poverty and powerlessness'? Workers in a few key industries maybe have access to the heart of capital, but many do not. We've seen the situation of unprofitable companies where militant action can win nothing except closure and loss of jobs. Where does the power lie in such cases? The capitalist system doesn't reside in the local council chamber, but it doesn't reside in an individual firm's boardroom either. Marx advised workers that in their struggles in the factories they 'ought not to forget that they are dealing with effects, but not with the causes of those effects', and that they should extend the struggle beyond the factory and make demands other than purely economistic demands for better wages.[9] Reproductive action such as we've described around housing in Lambeth is often criticised for being parochial and isolated – but are not unofficial strikes too sometimes isolated and vulnerable, especially those in low-paid women's work? How much more power have women night-cleaners in the Shell Centre in Waterloo than, say, the women of Ferndale Court in Brixton on rent strike in support of their demand to be moved to permanent accommodation? Indeed the cleaners have less nuisance value: cleaners can be sacked and replaced overnight. The women in Ferndale Court would go nowhere unless the council themselves move them – and that was their very demand.

For years revolutionary parties of the left have neglected all forms of action but those of the factory floor: because in the employer you come up against the real class enemy, directly, in person. Not only is this crude, it is wrong. Many workers in their place of work are up against no fanged demon of capitalism but a benevolent head teacher, a petty-minded park superintendent or a mild professor, whose status as class enemy is difficult to realise. At home, on the other hand, they are up against the landlord and the hire purchase credit chaser whose part in capitalism is clear enough. The analysis has to be more comprehensive.

To organise at the workplace alone leaves out half the *worker's* own experience of exploitation – speaking as it does of the cash wage but not of prices or of the social wage. More important, it excludes all *wageless* people from organisation. Pensioners, women doing unpaid domestic work, students at school and college, the unemployed and the invalid collecting state benefit – such people are a political resource, needed in struggle and needing it too. Reproduction, whether it be the practical reproduction of labour power or the ideological reproduction of our class system, our relationship to capital, is something in which everyone is involved.

Industrial struggle in the key industries is still the heart of the labour movement and will remain so. But, if the movement is to continue to gather strength in the contemporary phase of capitalism, others must be drawn into it and their different struggles recognised and joined by industrial militants.

Collective action about services

We are used to talking about struggle at the *point of production*. We know what it means – it is easy to envisage the factory floor, the building site or the office. One reason it is so easy to see is that it nearly always implies a place. The point of *collective reproduction* is not so easily pinned down. In some of its aspects it is of course a place too: housing takes place in a distinct location, and a council estate is a territorial unit. But private tenants renting from the same landlord (take the Gerson Berger case in Lambeth) may live miles, even cities apart. Education takes place in identifiable schools and colleges. But social casework and social security are delivered to people as individuals, sometimes at home, sometimes across a counter.

In spite of the intangible nature of the process of collective reproduction, many struggles *have* been developing around it in recent years. Some are easier to organise than others. We've seen several instances of housing struggle in Lambeth. The fact that all people claiming social security benefits in a certain area obtain them through one office has enabled claimants to contact each other and form claimants' unions, of which there are now very many in Britain. Action around demands for nurseries and other forms of child care have been organised by local Working Women's Charter and other groups. Schools have presented a problem of organisation, because parent-teacher associations, even in working class schools, are often dominated by more well-to-do parents. But the scope for change is there – aided in primary schools by the fact that mothers meet each other outside the school gates. Health services are specially difficult to organise because patients are usually preoccupied with personal problems to the point that collective action is inconceivable to them. Besides, the catchment area of hospitals is very large. Some women, however, have been forming health groups, often starting by learning how to administer their own pregnancy tests and understand their own (physical) reproductive problems.

The last five or six years have seen a rapid growth in collective action of this kind and two conclusions have been drawn and are beginning to be acted upon. One is that trades unions and rank and file groups have been for too long unconscious of the importance to them of the social wage and the need for them to go out of their way to contact and support such struggles. The second is that a natural connection exists between the interests of state workers and state 'clients'.

One of the strengths of community workers, arising from their employment in the town hall, is that they are able, theoretically now, perhaps increasingly in practice, to generate these contacts between the waged and those who are often wageless.[10] Community workers, even more than other professions, have to fight against isolation, professionalisation and the brand of philosophy that is favoured by their supervisors. Those interviewed in Lambeth, however, recognised a clear need for mutual and union support for their work and a collective forum in which to work out the theory of their position. So long as a way could be found to overcome the individual, isolated style of work, the scope for political action could be considerable.

What of *elected members* of local councils? They characteristically intervene in collective reproduction, because that is the main work of the committees of council on which they serve. In the foregoing chapters we've seen something of the difficulties of their position.

Much liberal democratic literature and practice makes a sharp distinction between bureaucrats and politicians. It is implied: if one could just put more power into the hands of the elected member and weaken the officers' grip on policy, all would go very much better for working class interests. This is at one and the same time a misinterpretation of the position of members, and of that of officers. Many 'officers' are also 'workers' and identify as such. Conversely, it is far from evident that all elected members are politically distinct from senior officers in the bureaucracy.

Evidence from Lambeth has shown a close partnership between senior office holders of the two sides, drawn even closer through the mechanisms of corporate management. In the housing field their predispositions in matters of policy are not dissimilar. As far as the public can see they stand shoulder to shoulder. This is not a phenomenon unique to Lambeth but is a characteristic of social democracies in modern capitalism.[11]

The story of Lambeth has yielded many examples of the impotence of the local Labour leadership radically to change the circumstances of the working class population. But if the leadership is inexorably caught up in the procedures of the state and the management of the economy, what, all the same, of the back-bencher? Many ward councillors are people who have stood for election, even taken the step of joining the Labour Party, just for the advantages they hope it may give them as advocates or representatives of local working class interests. Once in the party and the council chamber the impediments standing in their way are many.

Corporate management has meant that the backbencher, the ordinary ward councillor, is further from the sources of decision and power (such as they are in the town hall) than ever before. He* is excluded by the high-level partnership between leadership and senior officers and takes little part in the policy planning process. The ward councillor can do little more than dutifully present petitions or try to rustle up a little support for action among other backbenchers in Group, where he can pull off an occasional coup. 'If there were more like me, we could mandate the leadership to do what we want.' Since there are not – his only weapon is the moment of weakness in the party and his only tactic operating in the Whip's blind eye.

He can attempt to attain to the leadership – but he will have first to prove that he speaks their language. He can try merely to influence them. But the promises they give him will be worth little more than those they give the working class group itself. Besides, 'if

---

* Men predominate among councillors. In Lambeth at the 1974 election 52 men were returned as against 8 women.

one is not otherwise powerful, one's presence in the smoke-filled room or in the air-conditioned office is tolerated only for so long as one is congenial company. One soon ceases to be congenial company if one's insistent contribution to the proceedings is, howsoever delicately and diplomatically, to unite the same old bundle of stinking rags and say "I want something doing about these".' This was the experience of Norman Dennis, a backbench councillor and activist.[12] Jon Davis, who also began as a community activist and moved to a position of influence in the local council's Labour Group, is clear-cut about the unlikelihood of either sympathy or effective support for working class action from councillors. 'The role constraints of local councillors, and not some inherent character defect, make it more than probable that they will be at least wary of and more likely actively hostile towards community activists.' He points to a natural competition between councillor and activist for community support; the pressure on the elected member of the party line and party loyalty; and the effect of being 'simply frozen out of all the patterns of information flow and the perpetual brokerage that constitute the political aspect of local government'.[13]

Many activists have of course kept out of the council and of the Labour Party because they have decided that the council structure presents a zero-sum game: to achieve significant change in policy one must be in power; once in power one is by definition part of an apparatus of state and a manager of public affairs, unable, and increasingly unwilling, to change policy. To be a councillor is to accept the agenda of the council. The principles underlying this agenda are management ones. It defines matters in terms of the possible, while working class demands are, and have to be, 'unreasonable'.

It is seldom that a left-wing captures power on a majority group in a local council and when they come near to it, as in Lambeth in 1971, they do not remain for long undiluted by the right. The Norwood constituency returned 15 councillors at the 1971 election, representing a sizeable left-wing influence both on the composition of the leadership and on policy for a short while.

By 1974 their position had dwindled to that of gad-fly to a leadership that was 'as solid right-wing as anything outside the East End'. Given the role of the Whip, the drama between the left and the leadership has to be acted out not in public but in Group. It is a drama in which the working class population are not themselves involved and of which they are largely unaware.

To return to the isolated backbench councillor: he can of course take part directly in the action, as some in Lambeth were doing, working, with squatting groups, opening up houses and putting in homeless families; founding tenants associations; working with women's centres and so on. Such a councillor has the advantage over an outsider (though not necessarily over a council *worker*) of having accesss to council information which he can pass to groups.

Several activists and community workers interviewed in Lambeth felt involvement of councillors in housing action to be not only ineffective but actually counter-productive. Their experience had convinced them that councillors' intervention has bad effects on both action and organisation: sometimes it delays direct action, de-fuses energy, blocks the view of the problem — limiting its definition to matters the councillor can or is willing to see as within his scope, or that of local government. It increases the tendency to believe that someone else, specifically someone in authority, alone can solve the problems of a situation that in reality is a reflection of an entire mode of production and balance of class power.

Certainly the left-wing councillors in Lambeth, in espousing community development, do not appear to have questioned very deeply its uses to state as well as people. And those who worked with squatters appeared to take it as given that the ideal would be for extensive co-operation between council and squatting groups. A difference in goals and commitment became evident at the point that the council's new licensing proposals were made. While most squatting organisations quickly rejected the proposal, the supportive councillors like the rest of the Labour group welcomed it. Because they did not share the squatters' experience neither could they share their scepticism. The councillors' priority, it could at that point be seen, had been to shift council policy – and to harass their own leadership. The priority of the squatters was to shift council policy – while maintaining squatting organisation, initiative and strength as a mutual defence in a situation of serious housing shortage.

There are many examples of struggles in the housing field that have foundered through the intervention of, and reliance upon, the Labour Party, the electoral process, the Labour Group on council and on individual councillors. None is more painful or cautionary than the history of the St. Pancras Rent Strike of 1960 where tenants brought defeat upon their cause by subordinating their immediate goals to helping the Labour Party win a council election. The existence of a strong left-wing caucus in the party was unable to avert the tenants' betrayal.[14]

It is interesting, finally, to compare the two relationships the councillor has with the working class: that with the local population and that with the council worker. While he may be advocate for the working class population of the borough, it is very much less likely that he will develop solidarity with the council worker. By definition he cannot (he is not allowed to) be a worker within the town hall, sharing in organisation and action in that workplace. On the Joint Committee that manages industrial relations in the Whitley system to which the councils conform, the councillor is invariably on the *management* team.

This account of the difficulties faced by elected members will be confirmed by many who've experienced them – but who may nonetheless insist that it is possible to find ways of furthering working class struggle in matters of collective reproduction from within the council chamber.

On the local state's payroll

The second place of reproduction struggle is in the state's own workplace: offices, swimming baths, parks, building sites and day centres. This includes not just local council departments but other (non-elected) local state agencies that play in whole or in part a reproductive role. Examples are the urban transport services, the hospitals and so on. We can also include national state jobs of a reproductive kind where they take a local form, such as work in employment exchanges, social security offices, the post office (Giro, family allowances).

The state, like industry, is hierarchical. At the top are senior officers, who take a big hand in making state policy (though convention has it that they subordinate themselves to politicians in this respect). In the middle ranks are the professional-style jobs of social workers, teachers, public health inspectors, rent officers. And at the bottom are the low-paid jobs of clerks and manual workers. To take social service department staffs as an example, in 1974 there were 5,000 senior bureaucrats; 20,000 field workers and no less than 82,000 'dishwashers, residential, etc.' out there in the children's homes of Britain.[15]

We saw in Chapter 1 how the early phases of management reform in local government introduced a set of techniques for tightening up the productivity of manual workers. Later phases of corporate management brought more comprehensive manpower planning and staff development policies which affected white-collar workers. Indeed, the bureaucracy of the local government trades unions have to some extent co-operated in this strategic planning of the labour force. Since the cutback in public expenditure and official anxiety about the rocketing payroll of local councils they have collaborated with the employers, through the Whitley Council mechanism, in a Joint Manpower Watch which collects and analyses statistics of local authority employment.[16]

It has been a characteristic of reproductive jobs of the local state, jobs in social services, health services, housing, education and so on, that they have become increasingly routinised, disciplined and de-skilled. This is what people mean by 'the social factory'. Employees of the state, as well as those who receive its services, have felt less and less in control of the processes of welfare. In education the creativity of both teacher and child is subordinated to streaming, grading and exams. In colleges and universities education is lost in training geared to the needs of employers. In the hospitals patients often feel they are treated as social equipment, rather than human beings, and for their part doctors, nurses and auxiliaries feel they are cast as maintenance engineers. The institutions of the welfare state have been 'established closer to the production system. The schools and colleges, the welfare system, the new housing estates were all made subordinate to the needs of capitalist production. This was achieved by applying the mode of that production — standardisation and profitability — to social life outside the factory.'[17]

In the state, as in modern industry, growth and development have necessarily led to more 'proletarianising' of employees.[18] They are more clearly *workers*. In the nature of capitalism, though, its gains bring about its losses. The state's professionals also *feel* more like workers, and so there has been a rapid growth of union membership and activism during the sixties and seventies. Before the War, NALGO (the National Association of Local Government Officers) was a Conservative-led professional club, to whose members the idea of trades unionism, let alone strikes, was anathema.[19] Now it is a mass-membership union and since the NALGO Action Group was formed in 1970 it has a rank and file of growing strength organised around shop stewards. NALGO cost employers about 100,000 days of work by industrial action in 1974. Even Lambeth has experienced its first overtime ban. The seventies also saw a growth of militancy in unions representing state manual workers with long national strikes of dustmen, postal workers, etc.

The return of a Labour government in 1974 did little to reduce worker pressure on the wage. 'Militant action among public sector workers, traditionally low-paid and less under the control of union bureaucracies, gained large wage rises and further raised public expenditure. The National Institute of Economic and Social Research, February 1976, calculated that this added £400–£700m. to public expenditure in 1974–75.'[20] Straightforward wage demands are one arm of the pincer movement of workers on the state. The other is pressure for the maintenance and increase of expenditure on education, health and housing. The understanding of capitalist reproduction both explains and endorses something that had begun to characterise the actions of local state workers: the inclusion of these qualitative issues (of the nature and standard of services) in their demands alongside quantitative ones (of pay).

The dramatic cutback in public expenditure imposed by the government in 1975 and 1976 has had the effect of impressing upon many state workers the unity of interest of the worker as employee of the state and as client of the state. It is starkly clear that the existence of 50,000 posts in local councils standing unfilled and a threat of redundancies to come means both fewer jobs and deteriorating services.

The high proportion (56 per cent) of women workers in state jobs sharpens this awareness. The perception that many women have of the connection between state job and service 'client' is made more acute by the fact that they themselves are often both worker and client. A national women's organisation is emerging within NALGO. NALGO women in Hackney have linked up nursery workers with mothers in a campaign over nursery provision. In other boroughs social workers have taken direct action over home-lessness, refusing to put families into bed-and-breakfast hotels and squatting them, instead, in the council offices. We've seen the uses in Lambeth of the Public Health Inspectors organising into a London Action Group to use their knowledge of the law of public health against urban management authorities that, in another context, employ them. On the bigger scale, NUPE have been in the forefront of the fight against private pay beds in the hospital service. Maybe the next step will be (as in Italy) bus drivers and conductors refusing to collect fare increases, rent officers taking action in support of rent striking tenants and so on.

There are two strong reasons why, in their own interests as *workers*, local state employees are finding it necessary to include issues of reproduction (the nature of the service they are asked to perform) with their wage demands. These reasons are quite apart from the fact that, when at home, they are also clients. First, unlike workers in private firms, they cannot point to the company's growing profits when asking for more pay. Their pay cheque comes from taxes, not profits. Second, when public employees strike it is often of real inconvenience to 'the public', who in one guise of course are workers in private industry. Unless state workers include along with their demands on pay and conditions demands relating to the quality of service to the working class, private industry workers may feel such action to be directed against them as much as against capital.[21]

Social workers and teachers are quickly radicalised by their exposure to poverty and oppression. They find that the job they are *supposed* to do, alleviate deprivation, educate children and so on, would require many times the money they are given to do it. As a result many of them come to recognise that their actual function in capitalism is quite different: social control and the management of reproduction.

Professionalisation sometimes works in a contrary direction to class consciousness among state workers. Seebohm and Younghusband and others[22] have urged professionalisation on social workers. Its uses are to cut off social workers from the client population, to encourage them to see themselves as part of an accepted specialist group on a par with doctors and lawyers. It also 'encourages the introduction of businesslike career structures, where correct and professional behaviour (such as detachment and controlled emotional involvement) is rewarded with advancement.'[23] Some social workers are finding that they need some form of mutual support, other than a professional association, if they are to understand their position and decide courses of action. It may be that other groups of professional-level workers in the state will develop a similar analysis. Town planners are an example of a group whose younger entrants are looking for a workable theory of their position and a class-based form of action. The nearer, however, the professional group is to policy-making (and town planners are deeply involved) the harder does it become to evade the grip of the professional's objective relationship to state and capital.[24]

Making over the family

We have no choice but to look to women, and to the family, as soon as we begin to examine the state. 'The state in its welfare aspects begins and ends with the family.'[25] A striking feature of the instances of working class housing action in Lambeth described in previous chapters is the key role that women played in them. This is in strong contrast to industrial action, where among union and rank and file activists women are as a rule greatly under-represented. In tenants' associations and street groups in Angell ward and elsewhere women were among the organisers.* Their involvement sprang direct from their experience in the home. The engagement of mothers in employment is usually provisional, being placed second to care of children and home. There is thus little time or energy left for organising at work. But hit by intolerable housing conditions, or by actual homelessness, a woman becomes the most likely member of the family to take defensive political action.

> It's got to be women, we're the only ones that can understand the problem. The men are out all day. Take the situation where I live. My husband would never have done anything about it. He didn't have to sit there with the rats running over his feet. They're out at work. Their minds are occupied with other things. If it's a health problem, *you* know it's *your* kids are going to be ill if nothing's done.[27]

A mass campaign against council housing policies in Lambeth in 1974 was sparked off by women, immigrants from the West Indies, who had got stuck (contrary to council promises) in supposedly temporary council tenements. They too were mothers who had become homeless and had seen what they considered their very reason for existing, the maintenance of a home and children, fundamentally threatened.

Struggle inside the family and outside of necessity go together. It was clear from interviews with women in Lambeth that for involvement in struggle in the street or on the estate, a shift in

---

* I have described elsewhere the motives and experiences of three of these women.[26]

attitude to housework, home and husband was both a pre-condition and a result. 'As I began to go out, things indoors seemed more trivial. Oh, things are never like they used to be here. I let things go now. It used to be well turned out, all clean.' It also had a profound effect on the confidence of the women involved, the way they thought of themselves. 'In those days I had no confidence, not for that sort of thing. When you start getting involved you find you're not a cabbage any more.' 'When it comes to it – now I know I'll fight.'

As Mariarosa Dalla Costa said, in a wider context, 'struggle demands time away from housework and at the same time it offers an alternative identity to the woman who before found it only at the level of the domestic ghetto. In the sociality of struggle women discover and exercise a power that effectively gives them a new identity. The new identity is and can only be a new degree of social power.'[28] Some who exemplify this are the battered wives of Brixton Women's Aid Centre who, in rebelling against and actually abandoning their role as wife and housewife, even if only momentarily, not only found a new idea of their own power but a new collective means of activating it.

In many ways the state and capital compete with us for definition of the 'family'. What they need it to be is not necessarily what we want it to be. Look at the state's manipulation of family in Lambeth. On the one hand the council depended upon women's self-definition of family to keep children from getting into 'care' and becoming a burden on the rates. But the state was also using 'family' as an administrative device to place some limit, even if an arbitrary one, on its housing responsibilities. Squatters were placed in the ludicrous position of having to find or beget a child (or get a doctor's certificate to prove that one of them was six months pregnant) in order to become a 'family' and qualify for rehousing – or indeed even to qualify as a recognised squatter. At no time did the council have a policy with regard to the housing problems of the single, i.e. non-family, people in the borough.

Again, family was necessary to the council as a measure of control, to avoid anti-social behaviour particularly on council estates. Where this failed and tenants were causing administrative problems to the council, they were invariably known as 'problem *families*', emphasising the breakdown in the family control function required by the state. The opportunist nature of the local state's approach to family, however, is illustrated by the fact that, when it suited it, as in the case of the Acre Lane reception centre for the homeless, fathers were quite callously separated from mothers and children. The cohabitation clause in social security also, of course, in Lambeth as elsewhere, forces men wherever possible into a 'family' role and into the financial maintenance of children of the women with whom they are in relationship.

The state sometimes uses the word community when family, or more strictly, women, is meant. 'The government's policy of unloading the burden of its cuts in the welfare state onto women, of keeping them at home through necessity, is a means of preventing them from seeking work and figuring in the unemployment statistics. Instead local authorities talk of progressive-sounding ideas such as returning the old to care within "the community" rather than in old people's homes and day centres. The "community" they have in mind is women.'[29] Both 'family' and 'community' thus have a strictly utilitarian function for the local state and the terms of its support for neither necessarily coincide with the particular need that the individual has of them.

From a slightly different perspective it is possible to see some of the things that local *capital* wants of the family in Lambeth. In the first place, capital has actually defined the very shape of the family. The geographical mobility of people in Lambeth, especially in the poor central and northern areas, is extraordinarily high. People do not move for the fun of it. They move because industrial capital (that provides or fails to provide jobs), finance capital and property interests (that provide or fail to provide housing) push and pull them. The capitalist economy has stripped the family down to its bare nuclear essentials. A sociologist taking a strictly conventional view of families writes that those which are 'highly integrated into a kinship network or into a community inhibit the social mobility of their members. They hinder geographical mobility (a necessity for the smooth functioning of the economy) for whole kingroups are too cumbersome to respond sensitively to the changing demands of the economy.'[30] The result is that families in Lambeth tend to be strictly nuclear families, stripped of their older or unmarried members. There is also a high proportion of unsupported mothers with their children. Because of their mobility it is reasonable also to assume that few of them has relatives living nearby on whom they can call for support. The deterioration of the position of women with this paring down of the family has been well documented by the women's movement.

The practices of a local South London employer afford an insight into a few more of the many working bonds between local capital and local families. Freemans is a mail order firm.[31] In 1975 it employed about 5,000 workers, of whom half were part-timers and most of these were working mothers. A high proportion of the full-timers were women too. Those who work in the company's two South London offices are the housewives and mothers of Lambeth and Southwark. The firm has made a deliberate policy of generous conditions of work. Though the pay is only average for this industry (which means low: 75 or 80 pence an hour), the management are understanding about mothers' needs for time off if children are sick, there is a discount store for the company's goods and so on. In other words the firm have adapted their employment policy to the local labour market they are exploiting. This, however, is only one-third of the story of Freemans' involvement with the family.

Freemans' second relationship with the family lies in its selling operation. A mail order firm operates from a central (highly computerised and technologically advanced) warehouse. Instead of having shops in the high street and a staff of waged sales girls, Freemans has recruited a force of 400,000 agents who do their selling for them. These agents are mainly housewives. They do their job for the company from home and do not think of it as work but as a hobby. They get 10 per cent on every order they take and a discount on their own purchases, but on average an agent makes only 43 pence a week. The women are asked to apply their own standards of integrity in choosing customers, so their feeling of responsibility to their customers protects the company against bad debts.

The third tentacle of involvement with the family is obvious: it is the family as consumer. The housewife-workers service the housewife-agents who in their turn sell to millions of housewife-customers from the glossy catalogue, exploiting one of the housewife's few means of self-expression: consumption. They get at the family wage packet through the letter box. The management state explicitly that mail order catalogues in the home allow the family to choose what is to be bought *as a family* – because of course it is very cumbersome for all the family to make the Saturday morning trip to the stores in the high street. The result for Freemans has been a boom business and soaring profits. Its £105 million turnover in 1974–75 (a relatively bad year) represented a 25 per cent increase in sales. The ratio of sales to wages bill and the ratio of profits to capital invested are remarkably high in this industry. At the pinnacle of this empire, a pyramid constructed of women, is a board of directors of nine men.

This is only an example, no more than illustrative. Though the workers are local people, the bulk of Freemans agents and customers live far from Lambeth, But other mail order firms operating similarly, with headquarters elsewhere, are at work in Lambeth. Scores of women on every estate in the borough carry the catalogue of one company or another.

So the family is different things to capital, to the state and to the working class. Capital sees the family as market and labour force. The state needs a residential institution for workers and their young – with a strong element of social control over such matters as workshyness, truancy and delinquency. Ideally we should be coupled – though it will settle if necessary for the one-parent family. State and capital combine, too, of course to design the physical accommodation that moulds our family shape. Building societies, property developers and local councils have reduced our housing possibilities to the nuclear family carton.

But what do WE want? We want personal space – people who

are near us but not oppressive. We want a possibility of genuine growth and learning through association that is fairly continuous over time. We want a base from which to link ourselves into many different collective groups, especially class groups, without being splintered between them all. We want supportive, practical working relationships, not predetermined by sex, or by age, or constrained by the physical space available to us. All these things conflict with the 'family' that the state and capital tend to make us. One requirement is shared: a family that is useful for capitalism is warm, caring and attached. And we want to be warm, caring and attached. This is the raw nerve of our struggle. In trying to make the family dysfunctional for capital, how do we avoid further hurting ourselves?

Nobody knows the answer but many people are looking for it. A few things have been learned already. First, that the sex relationship, the balance of power in marriage, is defined by capitalism. Many men and women are trying to live together without one being thought of as the property of the other, trying to make the sharing of domestic responsibilities less unequal and stereotyped. This transformation offers a starting point for reproduction struggles. Second, we are learning that if the state benefits from us isolated in our housework, each pouring out the sunshine from our family-sized packet of cornflakes, we can collectivise. 'We pose then as foremost the need to break this role that wants women divided from each other, from men and from children, each locked in her family as the chrysalis in the cocoon that imprisons itself by its own work, to die and leave silk for capital.'[32] Some parents are joining together to form playgroups for shared childcare. Food co-operatives are springing up for shared shopping. Understanding the part played by the family in capitalism is releasing us from the inhibition that such struggle for changes in family relationships is mere 'lifestyle politics'. Provided that these collective actions are a conscious part of a struggle to escape from an old ideology and to sharpen awareness of our real relation to capital and to the state they can be part of a wider political struggle. They not only strike at capitalism, they define socialism: we have to transform the relations of reproduction as part of the struggle for socialism to ensure that socialism does indeed eradicate patriarchy, at home and at work.[33]

Ideas and practice

As capitalism reaps its historical harvest of stress and conflict the dominant class needs to keep the initiative through ideas. The state has a big part in this. Its work in strengthening the dominant ideology has become of more importance the more working class consciousness threatens to evade it. We should not look for ideology in some separate form.[34] There is no battle of ideas, free floating in some sphere of its own. Ideology is embodied in institutions. 'A worker doesn't go to work because he thinks the way he does; he thinks the way he does because he goes to work.' All the institutions we've looked at have a strong ideological tendency within them, working alongside their practical purpose. Step by step as they produce the labour force they also reproduce class relations.

Take the family: it is for caring, but it is also for persuasion and teaching. Take the schools and colleges of local government: technically they reproduce and develop skills and capabilities for working life. But a steady hand on the lathe is no good to capitalism unless the mind that guides it has accepted its role as wage labour. The theoretical work of universities and research institutes is nuts-and-bolts work for capitalism, which needs a theory of its practice every bit as much as socialists need a theory of capitalism. But these theories also have an ideological purpose. Initially research tools, once established they filter down into common currency and serve to make reasonable to ordinary people the changes they see happening around them. A theory of participatory democracy explains and gives a context to the 'participation' we're asked to do in our local borough development plan. Systems theory, with its compelling emphasis on wholeness, connectedness and stability seems to explain and make reasonable to people the changes they are asked to undergo in the place they work or the way they are governed.

To struggle against dominant values in this field of culture and ideology may seem at first sight like a cost-free game, as though we have nothing to lose but our blindfold. The truth of course is that capitalist relations are not a separate field of struggle. We cannot change our ideas and our beliefs without changing our practice. The two are knit into one: each makes the other. Which comes first is as impossible to answer as whether the chicken comes before the egg. And to change practice is a painful and costly process. There are many women who will bear witness to the fact that the ideas implicit in women's liberation only become real when they are no longer just a set of ideas to be considered, toyed with, but are *one's own ideas*, matching in all respects one's experience of life. As that happens the nature of relationships invisibly changes too, and there is no going back. The costs have been paid before we had time to measure them against the gains. That is why struggle in this and all fields of experience has to be collective: otherwise the individual may pay too high a price.

The situation in which we practise is a set of contradictions. We need the family, capitalism needs it too: the two uses of the family are incompatible. We need services: capitalism needs us serviced. We need jobs: capital needs the work done. On the other hand – capital needs our participation, yet we use these openings in a way that can threaten capital. Capital can benefit from having us grouped into associations; but collectively we are strong. That our struggle seems to take place in contradiction should encourage us because we are seeing dialectically something that is real. The contradictions are not so immobilising as they seem, because in their particular shape and form they are always changing and so opening up new possibilities for action. Uncovering truth by stepping outside the conventional ideas of family, school, local government or electoral democracy makes it possible to see the present situation for what it is *and at the same time* to roll it onward so that new terrain comes into sight.

References

1. Gearing up to govern / pp.5–40

Place of publication is London or Harmondsworth unless otherwise indicated.

1. The science of work study resulted directly from the Scientific Management Movement among engineers in the USA toward the end of the last century. F.W.Taylor was a pioneer in the application of a scientific approach to the analysis of manual work to increase productivity.

2. J.W.Glendinning and R.E.H.Bullock, *Management by Objectives in Local Government*, Charles Knight 1973.

3. J.Argenti, *Corporate Planning*, Allen and Unwin 1968.

4. S.Aaronovitch and M.C.Sawyer, 'The Concentration of British Manufacturing', *Lloyds Bank Review*, October 1974.

5. R.Murray, *Multinational Companies and Nation States*, Spokesman Books 1975.

6. P.A.Baran and P.M.Sweezy, *Monopoly Capital*, Pelican 1966.

7. A.Glyn and B.Sutcliffe, *British Capitalism, Workers and the Profits Squeeze*, Penguin 1972.

8. M.Wheatcroft, *The Revolution in British Management Education*, Pitman Publishing 1970.

9. H.Rose, *Management Education in the 1970s: Growth and Issues*, a report published by the National Economic Development Office, H.M.S.O. 1970.

10. 'At the end of 1969 the BIM's Consulting Services Information Bureau had some 1,400 consultancy firms on its list.' M.Wheatcroft, *op.cit.*

11. R.L.Ackoff, *A Concept of Corporate Planning*, Wiley-Interscience 1970, is a compact guide to the subject.

12. See for instance S.Beer, *Decision and Control*, Wiley 1966.

13. S.Beer, *Brain of the Firm*, Allen Lane the Penguin Press 1972.

14. Royal Commission on Local Government in England, *Report*, (Redcliffe-Maud Report), Cmnd. 4040, H.M.S.O. 1969.

15. *ibid.*

16. Royal Commission on the Constitution, *Report* (Kilbrandon Report), Cmnd. 5460, H.M.S.O. 1973.

17. Royal Commission on Local Government in Greater London, *Report* (Herbert Report), Cmnd. 1164, H.M.S.O. 1960.

18. Committee on the Management of Local Government, *Management of Local Government* (Maud Report), H.M.S.O. 1967.

Committee on the Staffing of Local Government, *Staffing of Local Government* (Mallaby Report), H.M.S.O. 1967.

Study Group on Local Authority Management Structures, *The New Local Authorities Management and Structure* (Bains Report), H.M.S.O. 1972.

Scottish Development Department, *The New Scottish Local Authorities: Organisation and Management Structure* (Paterson Report), H.M.S.O. 1973.

19. Committee on Local Authority and Allied Personal Social Services, *Report* (Seebohm Report), Cmnd. 3703, H.M.S.O. 1968.

20. Department of the Environment, *The New Water Industry Management and Structure*, H.M.S.O. 1973.

Department of Health and Social Security, *National Health Service Reorganisation, Consultative Document*, May 1971.

21. See for instance, Department of the Environment circular 100/73, outlining co-operation needed between water authorities and local authorities.

22. Ministry of Housing and Local Government, *The Future of Development Plans* (P.A.G. Report), H.M.S.O. 1965.

Town and Country Planning Act 1968, H.M.S.O. 1968.

23. Committee on the Management of Local Government, *op. cit.*

24. Committee on the Staffing of Local Government, *op. cit.*

25. *ibid.*

26. An INLOGOV report notes the shift from phase two to phase three 'corporate planning and increased effectiveness', around 1969–70. Institute of Local Government Studies, University of Birmingham, *Occasional Paper* No. 5, 1970.

27. See the phraseology of the Bains Report (see **18** above) and for instance Stockport Metropolitan District, Joint Committee, *Report to the New Council*, 1973.

28. 'In the period of the mid-sixties local government expenditure was growing rapidly both in absolute terms and as a percentage of gross national product. National economic pressure forced local government to attempt to restrain the growth rates as did a growing awareness in local government that existing growth rates could not continue indefinitely . . . pressure upon resources implies critical choices and traditional systems of financial management did little to assist choice.' J.D.Stewart, *The Responsive Local Authority*, Charles Knight 1974.

29. The Stockport Joint Committee, *op. cit.*, provides a good illustration of awareness of the balance between cost and impact. They urge centralisation in the new authority to achieve economies of scale. 'In practice, inflation and the pressures for increased standards of service as well as the experience of previous reorganisations do not lead us to suppose that economies will be translated into rate reductions. However, if this is not to happen, it is imperative that they be translated into an increase in the effectiveness of the service provided.'

30. J.D.Stewart coined the phrase 'community planning' for this more-than-corporate approach 'concerned with planning to meet the problems and needs of the community within a specified area, irrespective of the particular organisation that might be involved'. J.D.Stewart, *op. cit.* See also **18** and **21** above.

31. J.K.Friend and W.N.Jessop, *Local Government and Strategic Choice*, Tavistock Publications 1969.

J.K.Friend and C.Yewlett, 'Inter-agency Decision Processes: Practice and Prospect', Institute for Operational Research Conference 1971.

32. J.K.Friend, J.Power and C.Yewlett, *Public Planning: the Intercorporate Dimension*. Tavistock Publications 1974.

33. *ibid.* See the case study of Droitwich.

34. J.Benington, *Local Government Becomes Big Business*, Community Development Project Information and Intelligence Unit 1976.

35. Department of the Environment, *Making Towns Better*, H.M.S.O. 1973.

36. The respective bodies in 1976 are the Association of Metropolitan Authorities and the Chartered Institute of Public Finance and Accountancy.

37. The Centre for Environmental Studies sponsored a working group under the chairmanship of F.J.C.Amos to study the educational developments needed in higher education to serve the new management and planning. *Education for Planning*, Progress in Planning, Vol.1 No.1, Pergamon Press 1973.

38. Among work originating there, see J.D.Stewart, *Management in Local Government: a Viewpoint*, Charles Knight 1971, and T.Eddison, *Local Government: Management and Corporate Planning*. Leonard Hill 1975.

39. *Local Government Studies*.

40. Local Government Training Board, *Training Recommendation No. 7: Management Development*, 1971.

41. For example the studies carried out by McKinsey and Co. Inc. for Liverpool Corporation and Kingston upon Hull and those of Booz Allen and Hamilton for the London Borough of Islington and the County Borough of Stockport, which were widely studied, quoted and emulated.

42. 'New Directions for Local Government'; and 'A New Approach to the Problems of Cities', both circulated by McKinsey and Co. Inc. c.1972.

43. Lambeth's corporate planners mostly came from backgrounds new to the town hall. One was a solicitor and two had first degrees in physics, followed in one case by experience in O & M and in the other by an MSc in Business.

44. I.Holden and P.K.McIlroy, *Planning for Profit*, Hutchinson 1973.

45. See J.Bray, *Decision in Government*, Victor Gollancz 1970.

46. R.A.W.Rhodes, The changing political-management system of local government, *Institute of Local Government Studies*, University of Birmingham. Paper to ECPR Workshop, 1975.

47. London Borough of Lambeth, *Housing in Lambeth*, 1969; London Borough of Lambeth, *Lambeth Housing – Into the Seventies*, 1969.

48. M.Harloe, R.Minns and J.Stoker, *Housing Advice Centres*, published jointly by SHELTER and the Centre for Environmental Studies, 1974, discusses the work and limitations of the Housing Advice Centres of Lambeth and other authorities.

49. This democratic privilege was under pressure in 1975. The backbenchers on the Policy Committee were traditionally voted for only by backbenchers. To tip the balance against the resulting left-wing influence, the leadership was trying to amend the rules to enable vice-chairmen of committees to be included among the voting constituency.

50. The Lambeth system was modelled on Programme Planning & Budgeting Systems (PPBS).

51. In interview.

52. He was not, as it turned out, however, the strong manager the new system called for. He was ousted in May 1973 for being, as the *Streatham News* put it, 'an insufficiently effective coordinator'. His going also represented a consolidation of the right-wing in the leadership.

53. An extra meeting of all committees to discuss the corporate plan was introduced in 1975.

54. The Bains Report was criticised by many members for being an 'officers' charter'. But see for instance T.Eddison, 'New Deal for Councillors', *Local Government Chronicle*, 2 March 1973, and J.D.Stewart, 'Politics: the Greatest Gap in Bains', *Municipal Review*, No.514, October 1972. Both authors are pioneers of education for corporate management.

55. NALGO Action Group is a militant rank-and-file organisation within this union of local authority workers.

56. APT & C Grade.

57. Lambeth Borough Council, *Community Plan 1974–79*, Vol.7.

2. Local government as local state / pp.41–66

1. K.Marx and F.Engels, *The German Ideology* (1846), Lawrence & Wishart 1970.

2. Cuba, for example, has introduced a system of local electoral democracy with mass participation which makes an interesting comparison. C.Cockburn, 'People's Power: the New Political and Administrative System in Cuba', Centre for Environmental Studies Working Note 435, 1976.

3. See K.Marx and F.Engels, *The Communist Manifesto* (first published 1848) and F.Engels, *The Origin of the Family, Private Property and the State* (1884), Lawrence & Wishart 1972.

4. V.I.Lenin, *The State and Revolution* (1917), Peking, Foreign Languages Press 1976.

5. From an analysis by Lambeth Borough Council, Directorate of Development Services, *Report* BPL/RD/ARP/42.05.471 of April 1975. The Socio-Economic

Groups are as follows, A is SEGS 1, 2, 3, 4, 13; B is SEGS 8, 9, 12, 14; C is SEGS 5, 6; and D is SEGS 7, 10, 11, 15, 16 and 17.

Note: A: includes employers and managers in central and local government, industrial and commercial establishments both large and small; professional workers whether employers or employees. B: foremen and supervisors of manual workers, skilled manual workers and own account workers (such as self-employed persons in trades, personal service or manual occupations). C: non-manual workers exercising general planning or supervisory powers in non-manual occupations, and junior non-manual workers – those engaged in clerical, sales, non-manual communications and security operations. D: Unskilled manual workers, personal service workers, members of the armed forces (and occupations inadequately described).

6. Lord Redcliffe-Maud and B.Wood, *English Local Government Reformed*, Oxford University Press 1974.

7. In this section I draw on N.Poulantzas, *Political Power and Social Classes* (Part IV), New Left Books 1973.

8. 'In order concretely to take on this relative autonomy which, inscribed in the play of its institutions, is what is precisely necessary for hegemonic class domination, the state is *supported* by certain dominated classes of the society, in that it presents itself, through a complex ideological process, as their representative: it encourages them in various ways, to work against the dominant class or classes, but to the political advantage of these latter.' N.Poulantzas *op. cit.* p.285.

9. R.Miliband, *Parliamentary Socialism*, Merlin Press 1972.

10. R.Miliband, *The State in Capitalist Society*, Quartet Books 1969.

11. R.Miliband, as **9** above.

12. 'It is often held that parliament presents itself to the dominant classes as a place of danger . . . it is, generally speaking, a myth.' N.Poulantzas, *op. cit.* p.313.

13. D.Skinner and J.Langdon, *The Story of Clay Cross*, Spokesman Books 1974. R.Minns 'The Significance of Clay Cross: Another Look at District Audit', *Policy and Politics*, Vol.II, No.4, June 1974.

14. *Labour Research*, 'State and Industry: a New Partnership', January 1976.

15. R.Miliband, as **9** above.

16. J.Benington, *Local Government Becomes Big Business*, CDP Information and Intelligence Unit 1976.

Canning Town to North Woolwich, the Aims of Industry? Newham Community Development Project, 1975.

Jobs in Jeopardy, a Study of Job Prospects in Older Industrial Areas, CDP Information and Intelligence Unit 1974 (reprint).

17. Current research by J.Thornley and R.Minns at the Centre for Environmental Studies, sponsored by the Social Science Research Council, examines public authority/private enterprise shareholding schemes.

18. In this section I draw on L.Althusser, 'Ideology and Ideological State

Apparatuses', in *Lenin and Philosophy and other Essays*, New Left Books 1971.

19. A useful discussion of this theme is E.Wilson, 'Women and the Welfare State', Red Rag pamphlet No.2, 1974.

20. As **18** above.

21. T.Bunyan, *History and Practice of the Political Police in Britain*, Julian Friedmann 1976.

22. A.Gramsci, *Selections from the Prison Notebooks*, Lawrence & Wishart 1971 (written between 1929 and 1935).

23. *ibid.*

24. Conference of Socialist Economists, 'Women, the State and Reproduction since the 1930s', in *On the Political Economy of Women*, CSE Pamphlet No.2, Stage One 1976.

25. F.Engels, *The Origin of the Family, Private Property and the State* (1884), Lawrence & Wishart 1972.

26. Mariarosa Dalla Costa, *Women and the Subversion of the Community*, Falling Wall Press 1972.

27. Mary Farmer, *The Family*, Longman 1970.

28. *ibid.*

29. Conference of Socialist Economists, *op. cit.*; E. Wilson, as **19** above.

30. W.Beveridge, *Report on Social Insurance and Allied Services*, Cmnd. 6404, H.M.S.O. 1968.

31. Conference of Socialist Economists, *op. cit.*

32. Current and capital expenditure at current prices. Figures exclude debt interest to central government, and central government grants to public corporations.

The source for these and other figures given below is *National Income and Expenditure*, H.M.S.O.

33. Department of Employment and Productivity, *Gazette*. Figures are for Great Britain and exclude traffic wardens and some other small groups of workers. In 1974, 55·2 per cent of the total and 86 per cent of part-time workers in local government were women.

34. In the following paragraphs I draw on I.Gough, 'State Expenditure in Advanced Capitalism', *New Left Review*, July–August 1975.

35 S.Aaronovitch and M.C.Sawyer, 'The Concentration of British Manufacturing', *Lloyds Bank Review*, October 1974, No.114.

36. I draw in what follows on three essays in C.Pickvance, ed. *Urban Sociology*, Methuen 1976. They are F.Lamarche, 'Property Development and the Economic Foundations of the Urban Question'; J.Lojkine, 'Contribution to a Marxist Theory of Capitalist Urbanisation'; and M.Castells, 'Theoretical Propositions for an Experimental Study of Urban Social Movements'.

37. A useful discussion is J.O'Connor, *The Fiscal Crisis of the State*, St James Press 1973.

38. Central Advisory Council for Education, *Children and their Primary Schools* (Plowden Report), H.M.S.O. 1967.

39. F.Field, *Poverty and the Labour Government*, Child Poverty Action Group 1969.

40. See *National Income and Expenditure*, Annual, H.M.S.O.

3. Management under pressure / pp.67–96

1. See Lambeth Borough Council, *Estimates*, for these years.

2. Lambeth Borough Council, *Community Plan 1974–79*.

3. The Brixton, Borough and Tooting employment exchanges are the relevant units, where the figure for registered unemployed rose from around 3,000 to around 9,000 between 1965 and 1972.

4. Shankland Cox Partnership and the Institute of Community Studies, *Lambeth Inner Area Study. Interim reports*, 1974.

5. Lambeth Borough Council, *Development Plan, Employment*, April 1975.

6. Lambeth Borough Council, *An Employment Policy for Lambeth, the Report of a Study Undertaken by a Working Party*, 1976.

7. A discussion of this regional policy for London and its effects can be found in D.E.C.Eversley, 'Old Cities, Falling Populations and Rising Costs', *G.L.C. Intelligence Unit, Quarterly Bulletin*, No.13, March 1972.

8. A summary of essential statistics for Lambeth will be found in Lambeth Borough Council, *Community Profile*.
See also Lambeth Borough Council, *Changes in the Socio-Economic Structure of Lambeth between 1961 and 1971*, BPL/RD/ARP/42.05.471 of April 1975.

9. As **4** above.

10. As **6** above.

11. C.Jackson, *Lambeth Interface*, privately published, 1974, gives a useful account of 'community action' in the early seventies.

12. In 1973 only 18 per cent of jobs in the borough were in manufacturing and construction, with 10 per cent in utilities and transport. The remaining 72 per cent were in distribution, finance and professional activities, public administration and other kinds of work. Source: 1973 Census of Employment, represented in Lambeth Borough Council, BPL/RD/ARP/42.05.471, April 1975.

13. *Angell* (newsletter), February 1974.

14. M.Harloe, R.Issacharoff and R.Minns, *The Organisation of Housing*, Heinemann 1974, contains a study of Lambeth's housing policy and organisation in the period of Tory majority.

15. For an account of the squatting movement in the country as a whole in this period see: R.Bailey, *The Squatters*, Penguin 1973.

16. Lambeth Borough Council, Housing Committee, *Report H.40/72–3*, 16 April 1973.

17. Lambeth Self Help Housing Association, Annual Report, *Squatting in Lambeth*, 1972–73.

18. The decline of the left's power in Group was more or less complete by 1975 when twenty-seven out of thirty of the committee offices were held by the right.

19. The activities of the neighbourhood councils and other progeny of the council's community development policy is discussed in Chapter 5.

20. The Vice Chairman of Housing (1971–73) said in interview that his political purpose was to split the Labour party and embarrass the council leadership. The Norwood group were in fact suspended from Group for three months in 1974 for flouting the Whip over a planning issue.

21. These figures are believed by housing action groups to be seriously under-stated.

22. Lambeth Borough Council, Housing Committee, Report HC.7/73/4, 18 June 1973.

23. In a small area of north-central Lambeth selected for the Department of the Environment's Inner Area Study the consultants' sample survey found that only a little over half of the households had lived at their present address for five years or more. Half of the 'movers' had come into the borough from elsewhere. 'Inner Area Study, People, Housing and District', Shankland Cox Partnership, September 1974.

24. Lambeth Borough Council, *Press Release No.648*, 1974.

25. Lambeth Borough Council, Agenda of Council Meeting, 10 July 1974, Item 9.12, Vacant dwellings in council ownership.

26. *ibid.*

27. *ibid.* 'In the case of tenants incurring serious rent arrears or disrupting an estate, a management transfer to a short life property on licence could be carried out until the position had been rectified.'

28. Greater London Council, *London Borough Council Elections*, 13 May 1971, compiled by the Intelligence Unit.

29. These figures are averages for the five wards in each constituency.

30. B.Hindess, *The Decline of Working Class Politics*, MacGibbon and Kee 1971.

31. The figure for March 1968 was 1,027 and for March 1974 1,595. Source: Lambeth Borough Council Public Relations Office.

4. The community approach / pp.97–131

1. J.K.Galbraith, *The New Industrial State*, Penguin 1969.

2. See Chapter 1 above.

3. A dispute has developed in recent years between liberals in the management sciences who have tried to show ways in which systems theory and its practical management applications such as OR can be neutral or even positively socially responsible in the way they operate in firms and critics who argue, on the contrary, that the language used and the voluntary nature of the definition of 'system', combined with emphasis on stability and continuity, make it very improbable that these new concepts and skills can do other than serve the continuation of the capitalist mode of production and the society that is built upon it. See articles by R.Ackoff, J.Rosenhead and others in *Operational Research Quarterly*, vols.25, 26 and 27 during 1974–75.

4. L.von Bertalanffy, 'The Theory of Open Systems in Physics and Biology', *Science*, Vol.III, 1950.

5. S.Beer, *Decision and Control*, Wiley 1966.

6. 'Requisite variety' is the term used.

7. F.E.Emery and E.L.Trist, 'The Causal Texture of Organisational Environments', in F.E.Emery, ed. *Systems Thinking*, Penguin Modern Management Readings, Penguin 1969.

8. J.Rosenhead, 'Networks – for Control or Self-management?' from Radio 3 talks 'Are hierarchies necessary?', *The Listener* 31 August 1972.

9. T.Burns and G.M.Stalker, *The Management of Innovation*, Tavistock Publications 1961.

10. D.Schon, *Beyond the Stable State*, Temple Smith 1971.

11. S.Beer, *op. cit.*

12. J.B.McLoughlin, *Control and Urban Planning*, Faber and Faber 1973.

13. R.L.Ackoff, *A Concept of Corporate Planning*, Wiley Interscience 1970.

14. Committee on the Local Authority and Allied Personal Social Services, *Report*, Cmnd. 3703, H.M.S.O. 1970.

15. *People and Planning*, H.M.S.O. 1969.

16. *Local Government Chronicle*, 26 January 1973.

17. Greater London Council, *The Swinbrook Case*, pamphlet, March 1973.

18. If in doubt of the management interests inherent in 'participation' we should look not only at who is demanding participation but who is offering it.

In Franco's authoritarian Spain for example. An article in a respected Spanish journal deplored 'a characteristic phenomenon of our post-Civil War era has been and continues to be, the almost complete absence in the majority of Spanish people of any desire to participate socially and politically in any aspect of the life of the country'.

On 10 March 1975, while the country was still in the grip of dictatorship a congress of journalists in Seville handed out prizes for the best articles on 'participation in city government' and Barcelona was awarded the accolade of most-participating city of the year: 25,000 activists in 104 associations. 'The collaboration is not always supportive to the Council, it also exercises constructive criticism,' said the mayor, Enrique Naso. *Cambio 16*, 31 March 1975.

19. Royal Commission on Local Government in England, *Report*, Cmnd. 4040, H.M.S.O. 1969.

20. Association for Neighbourhood Councils, 'The Need for Neighbourhood Councils in the New Local Government', paper, June 1971.

21. Royal Commission on Local Government in Scotland, *Report*, Cmnd. 4150, H.M.S.O. 1969.

22. Association for Neighbourhood Councils, *op. cit.*

23. Association for Neighbourhood Councils, 'Towards One Nation: a Nation of Good Neighbours', paper, 1973.

24. LG4/743/45 of 30 July 1974.

25. Among the state's roles is that of attempting to subdue class conflict and create cohesiveness in the social formation. The idea of 'membership' is crucial in the resolution of conflict. See G.Vickers, *Making Institutions Work*, Associated Business Programmes 1973.

'Community membership' of the population is needed by the local state, but it has to be membership of the right type of organisation, focusing on issues posed in such a form that the state can handle them. It has to have a structure and leadership to which the state can relate. What the state must avoid is organisations forming in the community that are of a basically working-class and class-conscious kind which might step outside the conventional ideology and make demands that would constitute a genuine threat to dominant class interests generally and to state management interests specifically. See Chapter 6.

26. Speech at Deptford Town Hall, 5 June 1974.

27. Working Party on Housing Cooperatives, *Final Report*, H.M.S.O. 1973.

28. Department of the Environment Circular 8/76.

29. H.F.Wallis in the *Local Government Chronicle*, 9 February 1973.

30. Recognition of how little they *knew* about the casual labouring class in Victorian London was the main source of anxiety to the dominant class. See Gareth Stedman Jones, *Outcast London*, Peregrine 1976.

31. T.R.Batten, *Communities and their Development*, Oxford University Press 1957.

32. Committee on Children and Young Persons, *Report*, H.M.S.O. 1960.

33. The FACs may be seen as the forebears of the Home Office Community Development Project through the part played in the creation of both schemes by the senior civil servant and reformer Derek Morrell.

34. Association of Community Workers, *Knowledge and Skills for Community Work*, 1975.

35. Aryeh Leissner and Jenifer Joslin, 'Area Team Community Work: Achievement and Crisis', in M.Mayo and D.Jones, eds. *Community Work One*, Routledge and Kegan Paul 1974.

The Home Office intention for FACs was that they should be 'the one door on which all could knock' and 'to diminish the need to receive children into or keep them in care', i.e. both humanitarian and practical penny-pinching. When, after some years of operation, the Home Office made a study of FACs they found that they were showing a clear tendency to regard *the community as the basic client unit* and to allot much time and effort to community work. The Home Office's experience of FACs had an important part in the development of local authority community work.

36. Calouste Gulbenkian Foundation, *Community Work and Social Change*, Longman 1968.

37. *ibid.*

38. *ibid.*

39. Susan Cooper in *Local Government Chronicle*, 16 March 1973. This is characteristic of Liverpool Corporation's approach to corporate management and community development.

40. For illustration of this new trade in social science see A.Shonfield and S.Shaw, eds. *Social Indicators and Social Policy*, SSRC, Heinemann Educational Books 1972.

41. Calouste Gulbenkian Foundation, *op. cit.*

42. D.V.Donnison, 'Micro-politics of the City', in D.V.Donnison and D. Eversley, eds. *London: Urban Patterns, Problems and Policies*, Heinemann 1973. See also R.Sennett, *The Uses of Disorder*, Allen Lane the Penguin Press 1970.

43. P.Bachrach reviews these earlier theories in *The Theory of Democratic Elitism*, University of London Press 1969.

44. See P.Bachrach, *op. cit.*, who develops a participatory theory. Also C.Pateman, *Participation and Democratic Theory*, Cambridge University Press 1970.

45. For instance, R.A.Dahl, *Polyarchy*, Yale University Press 1971.

46. See footnote on pp.44–45.

47. It is worth musing for a moment on the sources of this work. The Calouste Gulbenkian Foundation is known for its progressive policy of funding community work and community action. Yet its funds originate in finance dealing and the oil industry. It operates from Lisbon where it apparently found no difficulty in co-existing with the regime in Portugal throughout the Salazar dictatorship. These are persuasive reasons for looking for the advantage that may accrue to capitalism from community work.

48. Calouste Gulbenkian Foundation, *Working with Communities*, National Council of Social Service 1963.

49. As **31** above.

50. As **36** above.

51. Calouste Gulbenkian Foundation, *Current Issues in Community Work*, Routledge and Kegan Paul 1973. This was the report of a Study Group on Community Work 1970–73, the list of whose members reads like a Who's Who of community development. The support for the conflict method was not therefore an unrepresentative or minority position.

52. My emphasis.

53. On the search for responsiveness, see J.D.Stewart, *The Responsive Local Authority*, Charles Knight 1974.

54. For an outline of the method and the various projects see R.Burgess, 'Action Research in the UK', a paper from the Planning Intelligence Directorate Department of the Environment, 24 June 1975.

55. Central Advisory Council for Education, *Children and Their Primary Schools*, H.M.S.O. 1967.

56. The official report of this project was *Educational Priority*, H.M.S.O. 1972.

57. E.Midwinter, *Priority Education*, Penguin 1972.

58. *ibid.*

59. Properly I should spend time here discussing the Urban Programme as a whole. Introduced by Callaghan in 1969 a Local Government Grants (Social Needs) Act permitted the Home Secretary to 'make payments to local authorities who incur expenditure by reason of the existence in any urban area of special social need'. This was the framework from which the national CDP experiment arose, and the two were later administered from within the same Community Programmes Division of the Home Office. The Urban Programme funded many hundreds of small community action and community development projects in the last five years, from summer playschemes to community law centres. Much of interest could be learned from studying it in detail and from looking at the work of the Urban Deprivation Unit in the Home Office.

60. Source documents here are internal Home Office papers and press notices, 1970.

61. Home Office, 'CDP: A General Outline', paper, 1970.

62. P.Marris and M.Rein give a detailed analysis of the US poverty initiatives in *Dilemmas of Social Reform*, Penguin 1967.

63. Also the Northern Ireland Ministry and Commission for Community Relations, whose relationship with the community work programmes of the British Army and Royal Ulster Constabulary is described by H.Griffiths in 'Community Development in N.Ireland, a Case Study in Agency Conflict' (unpublished paper), 1974.

64. Community Development Project Information and Intelligence Unit, *The Inter-Project Report*, 1974.

65. Commission of European Communities, 'Pilot Schemes and Studies to Combat Poverty, UK Section', paper, November 1975.

66. R.Batley, *The Neighbourhood Scheme: Cases of Central Government Intervention in Local Deprivation*, Centre for Environmental Studies, RP 19, 1975.

67. Home Office press notice 18 July 1974.

68. *The Guardian*, 9 September 1974.

69. Discussion document accompanying letter from S.T.Garrish, Department of the Environment, to local authorities, 4 September 1974.

70. The Home Office Community Development Project cost no more than £5 million and the Urban Programme as a whole only between £3 and £6 million a year. The sums reaching local areas were negligible in comparison with local government budgets.

5. Whose initiative? / pp.132–157

1. In 1969 the National Executive Committee of the Labour Party introduced a scheme for giving more voice to the party's rank and file. It was called *Participation '69*.

2. Meeting of the Neighbourhood Councils Sub-Committee, 9 May 1972, reported in Lambeth Borough Council, Report P8/72–73 Appendix M.

3. Lambeth Borough Council, *Community Plan 1974–79*, Vol.7, General Administrative and Support Services Programme Area.

4. Semi-official elections of this kind were the basis of Golborne ward neighbourhood council in Notting Hill in 1971.

5. Details of the organisation and work of the ten neighbourhood councils can be found in *Lambeth: Neighbourhood Councils 1971–74*, a paper prepared by the Neighbourhood Councils Office, Lambeth Borough Council.

6. 'Neighbourhood Councils and their relation with the Neighbourhood Councils Sub-Committee and with the directorates and service committees of the council.' Lambeth Borough Council, Report P.8/72–73, Appendix M.

7. *ibid.*

8. Report by the Chairman of the Neighbourhood Councils Sub-Committee. Lambeth Borough Council, Report P.8/72–73, Appendix I.

9. Note of a discussion at Policy Committee Special Meeting, Wednesday 28 February 1973. Lambeth Borough Council, Report P.8/72–73, Appendix K.

10. Letter dated 18 July 1973 from the Chief Whip of the Majority Party, Lambeth Borough Council, to Chairmen of Neighbourhood Councils.

11. Paper by the four Neighbourhood Council Development Assistants, May 1974, included in *Lambeth: Neighbourhood Councils, 1971–74*, prepared by the Neighbourhood Councils Office, Lambeth Borough Council.

12. 'Role and Objective'. A paper prepared by community workers in Lambeth Borough Council, Directorate of Social Services, 1974.

6. The new terrain of class struggle / pp.158–184

1. A.Gramsci, from C.Boggs, *Gramsci's Marxism*, Pluto Press 1976.

2. B.Greaves, 'Communities and Power', in P.Hain, ed. *Community Politics*, John Calder 1976.

3. S.James, 'A Woman's Place', in *The Power of Women and the Subversion of the Community*, Falling Wall Press 1973.

4. B.Greaves, *op. cit.*

5. *Morning Star*, 10 and 11 February 1975.

6. S.Hebditch, 'Ideology of Grass Roots Action', in P.Hain, ed. *Community Politics*, John Calder 1976.

7. Camden Community Workshop, *Report*, 1972.

8. I.Gough, 'State Expenditure in Advanced Capitalism', *New Left Review* 92, July–August 1975.

9. Jan O'Malley quotes this comment made by Marx when addressing London workers in 1865 in 'Community struggle in Notting Hill', awaiting publication.

10. M.Mayo, 'Community Development: A Radical Alternative?' in R.Bailey and M.Brake, eds. *Radical Social Work*, Edward Arnold 1975.

11. 'A whole parliamentary tradition of the working class movement has expressed its distrust of the executive power (a distrust due in particular to its idyllic illusions of the legislative) by interpreting these analyses as a challenge to the executive's legitimacy.

This has allowed them to make a cheap critique of the executive's predominance and to refuse to make an adequate critique of the capitalist state as such. . . .

In the framework of the capitalist class state, parliamentary legitimacy is not "closer to the people" than that legitimacy which corresponds to the predominance of the executive. In fact, these are always ideological processes in both cases.' N.Poulantzas, *Political Power and Social Classes*, New Left Books 1973, p.311.

12. N.Dennis, 'Community Action, Quasi-Community Action and Anti-Community Action', in P.Leonard, ed. *The Sociology of Community Action*, Sociological Review Monograph, No.21, University of Keele 1975.

13. J.Davies, 'Whose Grass Roots? Citizens, Councillors and Researchers', in P.Leonard, ed. *op. cit.*

14. D.Burn, *Rent Strike St. Pancras 1960*, Pluto Press for ARSE, pamphlet, 1972.

15. *Case Con* No.22, 1976.

16. Organised by the Local Authorities' Conditions of Service Board. For description of the workings of the Whitley system of industrial relations see B.White, **19** below.

17. 'What is Big Flame?' by the socialist revolutionary group Big Flame, Liverpool, informal paper.

18. J.O'Connor, *Fiscal Crisis of the State*, St James Press 1973.

19. B.White, 'Whitleyism or Rank and File Action', a NALGO Action Group pamphlet.

20. I.Gough, *op. cit.*

21. J.O'Connor, *op. cit.*

22. E.L.Younghusband, ed. *Education for Social Work*, Allen and Unwin 1968.

23. *Case Con* manifesto, published in R.Bailey and M.Brake eds. *op. cit.*

24. Professionalism has been important in the local state in the past in ordering and structuring its services, ensuring that dominant class interests 'as expressed through the bureaucracy' appear neutral and classless. Now, at the moment when socialist professionals are questioning professionalism, the state too is modifying professional roles in its key areas of adaptation. Unified corporate management depends on diminishing the power of the old professions, which led to restrictive practices. What is happening, however, is not a diminishing of professionalism in the long run but the normal progress of division of labour. What are in fact new specialisms (corporate management and community work will most likely become professionalised in coming years) appear first in the guise of generalisms.

25. E.Wilson, *Women and the Welfare State*, Red Rag pamphlet No.2, 1974.

26. In KNUCKLE, a monthly newspaper for workers and tenants in Lambeth and Southwark, we published in 1975 a series of articles based on interviews with and involving local women. They focused on their work and involvement in collective action. The one referred to here also appears in M.Mayo, ed. *Women in the Community*, Routledge and Kegan Paul, forthcoming.

27. *ibid.*

28. Mariarosa Dalla Costa, *Women and the Subversion of the Community*, Falling Wall Press 1973.

29. *Case Con* No.22, 1976.

30. Mary Farmer, *The Family*, Longmans 1970.

31. *As Things Are; Women, Work and Family in South London*, Dustbin Press, Union Place, 122 Vassall Road, London SW9 6JB, 1977.

32. Mariarosa Dalla Costa, *op. cit.*

33. Conference of Socialist Economists, *On the Political Economy of Women*, CSE Pamphlet No.2, Stage One, 1976.

34. L.Althusser, 'Ideology and Ideological State Apparatuses', in *Lenin and Philosophy*, New Left Books 1971.

Index

Vassall, 44,89; Neighbourhood
Council, 79,140,142,143,152,154,
157
Vauxhall constituency, 88,89,92

wageless, 166,168
Water Act, 13
water authorities, 14,46
welfare state, *see* state
West Indians in Lambeth, 71,78,177
Wheatley Commission and Report,
106
Whitley Councils, 172,173
Wilson, Sir Harold, 23
women, role in capitalist reproduction,
58–62; and local government, 58,
175; in paid work, 61,164,166,177,
180; home, family, 163,177–83; in
Lambeth, 71,75,95,177,180,181;
and social security, 56; battered, 95
Women's Aid Centre, 178
Women's Centre, 79
women's liberation movement, 59,184
Worcestershire County Council, 104

workers, 52,63; state, 46,63,101,126,
163,168, (in local government), 37,
38,62,67,103,172–76, (and 'clients),
168; *see also* officers; professional
workers
working class, and the state, 42,47; in
Lambeth, 43,44,67,69–75,82; and
corporate management, 37–39,158;
and community development, 153–
55; and community action, 159–61;
and electoral democracy, 1,2,47–49,
168–72; and Labour Party, 88,92,
93,110,171; and culture, 58; and
social services, 55,62; and research,
2; militancy, 9,18,50,72
Working Women's Charter, 167
workplace struggle, *see* production
struggle; reproduction, employment
in

Young, Michael, 106
Younghusband, Dame Eileen, 114,
115,176